About the author

Sharron Lowe began her career as a beauty consultant and ran national training teams before launching her own business coaching consultancy twenty-five years ago. Since then she has been the go-to coach for luxury brands, including Chanel, Calvin Klein, Clinique, Parfums Christian Dior, Estée Lauder and Lancôme.

Over the past fifteen years Sharron has also run image and confidence-building workshops with the charity Centrepoint, helping homeless young women get back on their feet. As a mentor in *Marie Claire*'s Inspire & Mentor Campaign, Sharron has reached thousands of people through an advice column.

Sharron has a phenomenal impact on the people she works with. She delivers results. It's that simple!

Praise for Sharron Lowe

'Sharron is one of the UK's top motivators and influencers, which is why we were thrilled to have her as a *Marie Claire* mentor. Reading *The Mind Makeover* is like having Sharron right by your side as you make the journey to change your life for the better.'

Trish Halpin,
Editor-in-Chief, *Marie Claire*

'Sharron is one of the most dynamic and inspiring women you could ever meet. Her energy and enthusiasm for life is infectious. Through her own success story and now with *The Mind Makeover*, she hands us the tools to burst through those imaginary barriers and reach a level of achievement and personal fulfilment beyond our wildest dreams. For Sharron, anything is possible; and this book will empower you to achieve anything.'

Sue Peart,
Editor of *YOU Magazine, Daily Mail*

'Sharron has this incredible ability to take someone from good to great. I have witnessed first-hand how she can drive a business forward by motivating people within the organisation to realise their potential by making the best use of their personal strengths. Throughout my career Sharron has been a fantastic coach and through her humour, energy and her focus on the positive, she has given me the courage and motivation to take on new and exciting challenges. I am so excited that many more people now have the opportunity to experience their own Mind Makeover.'

Lee Etheridge,
International Director of Education and Brand
Ambassador, Bare Escentuals

'Homeless young women lacking confidence and self-esteem leave at the end of Sharron's motivational workshop with the determination to turn their lives around. We are extremely grateful for the empowering workshops that Sharron has run for the past 15 years.'

John Raynham,
Head of Marketing and Fundraising,
Centrepoint Charity

the MIND MAKEOVER

THE ANSWERS TO BECOMING THE BEST **YOU** YET

SHARRON LOWE

piatkus

PIATKUS

First published in Great Britain in 2014 by Piatkus

A CIP catalogue record for this book
is available from the British Library.

ISBN 978-0-349-40180-5

Illustrations by D. R. ink
Designed and typeset by Paul Saunders
Printed in Great Britain by Clays Ltd, St Ives plc

Papers used by Piatkus are from well-managed forests
and other responsible sources.

MIX
Paper from
responsible sources
FSC® C104740

For the one and only Joe Lowe – my dad – with all
my love: you taught me many things, especially that
happiness is more within us than within things,
and that reality can always be beaten with imagination.
I'm blessed to be your daughter.

CONTENTS

ACKNOWLEDGEMENTS

Behind the achievement of any big goal there's a support team and I feel very grateful to mine. I affectionately call them Team Mind Makeover: they are the wonderful people who believed in my vision for this book and have made it possible to turn that vision into reality.

You would not be reading *The Mind Makeover* were it not for the luxury brands that I have been so blessed to work with as a success coach over the past twenty-five years. My clients and the thousands of people I have coached continue to be a source of tremendous pride and inspiration. When they tell me that the Mind Makeover principles have transformed their lives it's incredibly fulfilling. Their phenomenal results constantly motivate me to continue to coach and share the message and principles in this book.

I would like to thank the following people and organisations in particular:

My sister Annie was the first person to read my manuscript and has been the 'family editor'. Your unshakeable support, love and laugh-out-loud humour kept me highly motivated just when I needed it. As always, we two 'Lowe' girls stuck together through thick and thin.

Roger, who is always my number one fan, biggest critic and complete supporter of all I do. For the past year you have run every aspect of our lives so that all I had to do was to wake up and write. You did this so efficiently that I truly considered *not* telling you I'd finished the book so you'd continue and I could take a break! I'm blessed you're you.

I'm so very grateful to my wonderful friends and family for their love and support, and for putting up with me saying 'I'm busy writing' for a whole year, as well as listening to just one topic of conversation – *The Mind Makeover*! I so appreciate your supportive check-in calls and I'm so happy you're still here at the end of the writing journey.

Mum, for the past six years you have lived each day with the power of a positive attitude. Your immense courage and determination inspire me and I'm so very proud of you.

My publishers Little, Brown/Piatkus, who have made my first experience of writing and publishing a book a journey of constant improvement. Thank you for pushing me to 'step up' to the challenge that 'if we each did what we are truly capable of we would truly astound ourselves'. The team's belief, commitment and passion for *The Mind Makeover* are a constant source of inspiration to me. Claudia Dyer and Jillian Stewart have guided me through the rocky waters of editing to find the core of the Mind Makeover principles and create an empowering and very true-to-life book. Andy Hine and the Rights team have made *The Mind Makeover* available to a very big audience and for that I will be eternally grateful.

My agent Juliet Mushens, for being both funny and clever in all she does.

The young women I coach at Centrepoint (the UK's leading charity for homeless young women): your courage and tenacity to start your lives over again, and your positivity and sense of hope, are a lesson to us all.

And most importantly I'd like to acknowledge *you*, as you are the reason I wrote *The Mind Makeover*. My one goal is that what you are about to read guides, supports and encourages you in your very own Mind Makeover as you create your best life yet.

INTRODUCTION

Makeovers fill our TV screens, magazines and newspapers. We are encouraged to makeover our appearance, wardrobe, home, relationships, lifestyle, career … But no one encourages us to makeover the most important asset we have; the one that can have the greatest positive influence on us – our mind. By having a *Mind* Makeover you can empower yourself and enrich your life more than you ever imagined possible.

The Mind Makeover will show you how to move from where you are now in your life to where you want to be. It will be your guide as you take what it is you dream of having, doing and being, and turn it into reality. This is your personal 'how to' guide, packed with easy-to-follow strategies for success. This book will do exactly what it says on the cover – give you the answers you seek to live your best life yet. And don't doubt it for a minute – you can live the life you want.

❝ Within each person is the potential to build the empire of her wishes, and don't allow anyone to say you can't have it all. You can – you can have it all ❞

ESTÉE LAUDER (1908–2004)

from *Estée: A Success Story*

For many years I have been a success coach to global luxury brands, among them Chanel, Calvin Klein, Estée Lauder, Clinique, Parfums Christian Dior and Lancôme. I have spent thousands of hours coaching Mind Makeovers to the people who work for such brands. The strategies that make up *The Mind Makeover* (excuse the pun) have increased the success, happiness and fulfilment of countless individuals and, as a direct result, have generated millions of pounds in additional revenue for the luxury brands I coach.

Whether I coach just one person or present a Mind Makeover to an audience of over eight hundred, the impact and results are always thrilling and at times miraculous. Many people have told me that their personal Mind Makeover was life transforming and changed them into a better version of themselves. It got them to smash out of their comfort zone and stretch their perception of what they believed was possible. What they subsequently achieved and their results went far beyond their wildest hopes and dreams.

While I coach the Mind Makeover to many leading companies, the strategies are not designed solely for business executives or company employees – they can be used by everyone, whatever their goal in life. I also coach the

Mind Makeover principles to homeless young women at the UK charity Centrepoint, and, despite their circumstances, many start their life over again with a fresh, positive perspective. They retake school exams, enroll in further education, learn a new skill or start a career.

Does that inspire you and motivate you to want to try your own personal Mind Makeover? I certainly hope so. Here are a couple of statements that motivated me to write this book:

- If you always do what you have always done then you will always get what you have always got.

- Hell starts when the person you are now meets the person you could have become.

Do you want either of those statements to define how you see your life? No, I thought not.

So let's start the journey together now and work to release and maximise your belief, positive energy, desire, imagination, ideas, happiness, fulfilment, strengths, passions and success. If you want to live your best life yet and you want it strongly enough then what I'm about to share with you will be empowering, easy to do and lots of fun. And all those other makeovers – mere icing on the cake of life! A Mind Makeover will empower, impact and enrich your life far more. Trust me on this. As someone said to me recently after their own Mind Makeover: 'A mind lift is way better than a face lift! My life felt ordinary and it now feels extraordinary – all that was missing was my Mind Makeover.'

chapter one

YOUR VERY OWN MIND MAKEOVER

How would you describe your life right now? What would you say if I asked you 'How are you?'

Before you answer, take a moment and think about what most people would say if they were asked that question. If you stopped one hundred people on the street and asked them, 'So, how are you today?' Do you think the majority would answer with 'I'm fantastic thanks; my life's great'? Or do you think the majority would answer 'I'm fine' or 'I'm OK' in a bored, apathetic tone that lacks any passion?

When I hear the words 'I'm fine' I think of this simple mnemonic of the word 'FINE': Frustrated, Insecure, Negative and Exhausted! Why? Because more often than not it's a pretty accurate description of how that person really feels:

- **Frustrated** – they feel dissatisfied and unfulfilled with their lot in life

- **Insecure** – they do not feel in control and do not believe they can really have what they want

- **Negative** – they focus on what's wrong in their life and not on what's right

- **Exhausted** – they feel apathetic and lack energy, drive and passion

For too many people, saying 'I'm FINE' actually means they experience many of the emotions described above. Does any of this ring true for you, or do you know someone who fits this description? I'm sure you do. But *you* don't ever want to settle for a life that's OK or fine, do you? You deserve so much more.

Picture someone getting to the end of their life and saying to their family as they take their last breath, 'Well you guys, I asked you all to come here today so I can tell you that I've achieved everything I set out to achieve in my life. Early on I made the decision to aim for and get an average life. I chose to be steady, dull, boring and average, to never have the highs so that I then wouldn't have the lows. And I've pulled it off.'

You don't want your life to be 'average' – nobody does. We all want to live a life packed with passion, phenomenal experiences, amazing highs and adrenaline rushes. This is life as it should be lived. And yes, at times, we will also suffer lows, but these experiences are opportunities to learn and grow so we can then truly appreciate and enjoy the highs that we create.

So, before moving on, decide that you will not settle for accepting 'fine' for even one day of your life. Make each day count, as there's no such thing as an unimportant day. And here's why: you are fabulous now, in this very moment.

Having read that statement you will be thinking something along the lines of:

- Yep, I am fabulous (with a grin on your face); or

- I'm not fabulous – I'm just about OK, at a stretch.

If it's the latter then you need to change your focus away from what's wrong or lacking in your world. Start to be grateful for what you have now and not regretful for what you haven't got. Feeling fabulous will come from uncovering and then focusing, with all your will, on what's good in your life, because you can't have rosy thoughts about your future if your mind is full of the blues. In life, what's wrong is always available for you to think about – but so is what's right: your thoughts, your choice.

So recognise and appreciate all that's right in your life *now*. It's the only place to begin. It will help you fast-track to where you want to go and the journey will be quicker, easier and far more pleasurable.

FOCUS ON THE POSITIVE

Many people fall more easily and habitually into focusing on what's wrong – rather than on what's right – for them. It has become a habit to continually bemoan their lot in life and go for the sympathy vote. Often this is in the mistaken belief that thinking and talking about the negative aspects of their life will change things – but it doesn't work like that. If you relate to this, I want you to stop doing it (don't worry, I'll show you how).

Negative thinking will not help you and it will not give you the life you want. Focusing on the positive, on what you appreciate and what you are grateful for, is a far more effective way of changing your life for the better, so for just one day, today, try appreciating all your blessings. It's a habit that will enhance your life immeasurably. And if you're thinking 'that sounds good, but I don't have anything to appreciate and be grateful for that is fabulous', well stop right there. Of course there are some people who always want more, bigger, better, in everything from material possessions to relationships, holidays and jobs. But if you always look to the future you miss the joy of living in and appreciating the present moment.

> *Some people miss out on happiness, success and fulfilment, not because they never found it or had it but because they didn't stop and appreciate it when they did.*

If there was a fire in your home what would you rescue? A friend and colleague once had just such an experience. She told me 'it was horrific yet positives came out of it; I got to appreciate exactly what's important to me, my safety and health, my boyfriend and my cat' (I'm sure she said it in that order). 'I can replace material things and nothing can take my memories, even if the mementoes have long gone. The kindness and the support I got even from people I didn't know was life affirming and made me live in the moment and treasure what I'd stopped noticing and appreciating.'

Decide now to begin your personal Mind Makeover on a solid foundation of positivity – focusing on what is currently right in your life, and not on the negative aspects of it. Negative thoughts are like quicksand and you'll sink, pulled down by the things that are currently wrong or lacking in your life.

Focusing on what is wrong or talking about what's wrong, broken or missing from your world has no place in the coaching work I do or in your Mind Makeover. You only have to look at my client list to understand why I say this. The brands I work with don't need 'fixing' because they are not broken. Their energy is consistently positive and empowering and never negative. They recognise and celebrate previous successes and use their creative vision and imagination to see possibilities and opportunities that they can seize. How so? It's simple: people connected with these global brands make a conscious decision to expose and focus on how fabulous they are. They attack their days and their future with an optimistic, 'glass half full' approach. They anticipate a future bursting with new experiences, growth and positive change.

So here's the big question: do you see life in terms of a 'glass half full' or a 'glass half empty'? Do you have an optimistic take on your life or a pessimistic one? Think about the following statement:

> *When a pessimist is given an opportunity all they can see is difficulty; when an optimist is given difficulty all they can see is the opportunity hidden within.*

Recognising all that's right, feeling gratitude for it and celebrating it is a common-sense approach to living a happy and fulfilling life. Only by doing this will you be able to celebrate your fabulousness (I'm not sure 'fabulousness' is an actual word but I love how it sounds and how it can make me feel so I like to use it). But although a positive focus is a matter of common sense, many people fail to practise it in their own lives. Take a few moments here to think about this and how it relates to you and your life. You need to give yourself the time to think through things at all stages of your Mind Makeover. Why? Because the emotions that are evoked by doing this will empower and motivate you to take action.

You will not have all the answers now, but you will soon.

WRITE IT DOWN AND RECORD IT

Samuel Goldwyn, the famous Hollywood producer, told his film stars that 'a verbal contract isn't worth the paper it's written on'. When you keep a record you generate a more powerful effect than just keeping your ideas as thoughts in your head.

Make it a rule to write down and record your thoughts, ideas, visions and goals. If it's worth knowing or doing, then it's worth recording. Clarity is power.

Throughout *The Mind Makeover* I will ask you to do various exercises to empower you, give you clarity and get you to take action. Note: the exercises are not included because they're aesthetically pleasing or for my benefit (I already complete them regularly); their sole purpose is to stretch, challenge and motivate you to take action. This book will only become empowering, release your true potential and become life transforming when you put it into action, so please, do the exercises! As the great philosopher Socrates said, 'The unexamined life is not worth living.'

As you work through the book, write down your thoughts and answers in a notebook or journal, or on your computer or tablet. It doesn't matter where you write or how you write, simply that you do it. Know that every time you record your thoughts and ideas you are increasing your chances of moving from where you are now to where you want to be. It's a discipline and commitment that will serve you well. Regard recording your thoughts and ideas as your first step towards making positive changes in your life.

EXERCISE

What's your start point?

Answer these questions as fully as you can and reflect on all areas of your life: career, relationships, well-being, interests, family and friends.

- What in your life NOW feels OK?

- What in your life NOW feels good?

- What in your life NOW feels great?

You may change your answers as you work through the book and add new answers and make new points; however the key is that you have begun to focus and think about yourself and your life. You now have a clearer picture of your starting point and you have put yourself in the best place to begin your Mind Makeover.

To go from feeling fine to great, two things must happen: positive change and massive action. Or, you could put it in one word: movement. In life, change can feel scary but getting stuck is lethal. I love the saying 'change is inevitable but suffering over it is optional'.

POSITIVE CHANGE

Change brings about action, excitement, growth, discovery and new passions. It has been said that change is a blessing and a gift disguised in work clothes. Without change we limit our well-being in all areas of our lives. Change is a life constant just like breathing. The best change is that which you make happen yourself, as opposed to change that is forced upon you. Changes you create will dramatically increase your confidence and self-belief, and fast-track you to where you want to be.

Let me ask you a question: what if you always did what

you have always done and you always got what you have always had? How do you feel as you think through your answer to this question? Are you happy with your answer? Would that be enough for the rest of your life? Or do you want more? What if your life, as it is now, never improved and you didn't grow as a person? Would that be OK for you? No, I thought not.

Einstein said: 'Insanity is repeating the same actions time and time again and expecting a different outcome.' What thoughts and feelings does this statement trigger for you?

Inspiration and desperation

Do you feel inspired by this, or did your initial feelings of inspiration turn to feelings of desperation? Both feelings can be tremendous motivators, encouraging you to take action to achieve what you want. Knowledge of both inspiration and desperation is empowering and will give you a whole new level of control in steering the direction of your life. (You'll read more about this later.)

Decide to take responsibility for your life and use this book to get highly motivated to make positive changes. Do not blame others for the things you want but don't have yet. Don't wait for life or others to deliver your perfect life on a plate, they won't. Own it and decide to take full responsibility for yourself, your actions, solutions and goals right now. It feels fabulous when you do.

Massive action

You may have noticed that I used the phrase 'massive action' earlier. This is because there's no point thinking small here, as it won't serve you well. As someone said, 'Think big or stay in bed!'

Here's a powerful example of thinking big: 'When I was a child, my mother said to me, "If you become a soldier you'll be a general. If you become a monk you'll end up as the Pope." Instead I became a painter and wound up as Picasso' (Pablo Picasso).

You have an amazing capacity to move yourself from where you are now in your life to where you want to be. Remind yourself often that, if you always do what you have always done, then you will always get what you have always got. And keep in mind that other saying I first mentioned in the Introduction: hell starts when the person you are now meets the person you could have become. These two sayings motivated me to write *The Mind Makeover* and move outside what I had always done in my career (fabulous as it was). The important question is: what will these sayings and examples trigger inside you and in your life? Now there's an exciting thought, because when you decide that you want what you don't already have, you must begin to do what you have never done.

> *Knowledge has no power without action. Use it or lose it.*

WHAT DO YOU WANT?

Now it's time to think about specific goals. For example, do you want new or increased feelings of

- confidence

- happiness

- success

- fulfilment?

Or do you want things that you don't already have in your

- home

- career

- relationships

- finances?

Or, to do things that you don't already do, such as:

- commit to turning your ideas into a viable and profitable business

- learn to scuba dive

- join a gym and learn salsa dancing

- add a new language to your talents?

To achieve any of the things on your list you need to understand, without any doubt, that you must proactively change what you now do (your emotions, thoughts, behaviours and actions). This change can and will become a fantastic journey of discovery, filled with new experiences for you. Trust me, I've witnessed it thousands of times for those I coach.

So embrace change – make it your friend and not your enemy – and your results will be thrilling and maybe, for you, miraculous. Change is the catalyst to releasing your potential and making your life happier, more successful and more fulfilling for you.

When you are through with change, you're through!

WE'RE IN THIS TOGETHER

Happiness, success and fulfilment cannot be achieved alone. It takes a support team and the energy that comes from collaborating with others.

At the start of my consultancy business I became the success coach for a special project at the Royal Opera House, London and while I was there I often heard the following expression: 'However talented an individual in the orchestra believes they are, be very clear that no one can play a symphony alone.' This is also true in life.

That's where I come in. Everyone needs to be encouraged to live up to their potential, and this book will be your very own success coach to guide and support you on the journey that is your Mind Makeover. I want to inspire and challenge you (in equal measures) to create and live your best life yet.

Just take a moment and picture in your mind a single snowflake dropping from the sky in slow motion. It is so delicate that when it touches your hand it instantly disappears. Now imagine a thunderous avalanche crashing down a mountainside at a speed that is unstoppable. A snowflake is one of nature's most perfect and delicate objects but when lots of them join together they can create an avalanche. Then their combined energy and momentum creates an unstoppable force.

Think about other people who could support you. Who at work, at home or among your friends could add value to your life and help you to reach your goals and live your best life yet?

It's not only those people you already know who can be part of your support team. I've gained valuable support and motivation from some truly inspirational individuals by reading about them in their books and biographies. I have a library of support to back me up whenever I need it, and it can be as easy as opening a book to learn about and research new topics and life goals. There's a whole new team out there that you haven't even met yet. For example, I was recently a guest speaker at a *Marie Claire* magazine readers' careers conference. Three hundred people came together to network, form support groups and get new contacts. Opportunities surround us always. We just need to seize them.

> *When you choose not to seize opportunities it's the same as standing in the shade and complaining the sun isn't shining on you.*

WINNING STARTS WITH BEGINNING

You've laid the foundations of your Mind Makeover by doing the What's Your Start Point? exercise on page 10 and by thinking about what you want to change, so let's really get this journey started and work together to release, increase and maximise your belief, positive energy, desire, ideas, happiness, fulfilment, strengths, passions and success.

Whatever it is you want to have, to do and to be is all there waiting for you. All you need to do is to learn how to tap into your passions, talents and focus to live to your full potential.

This is personal. It is your own bespoke Mind Makeover and I'm going to show you how to:

- expose, recognise and celebrate all that's good in your life now

- expose and focus on your own unique fabulousness

- throw out any barriers to your future success

- use your thoughts to create your world

- program your thoughts for success

- smash out of your comfort zone

- dive into the world of your imagination

- learn to take control of your inner voice and make it your friend and not your enemy

- identify your energy diluters and enhancers

- create ambitious goals with a definite plan, and

- turn your dreams into your reality. *Now.*

All the above takes action, and to take action you need to get motivated. No one ever walked into happiness, success and fulfilment by doing nothing. Thinking about it won't work either. You need to decide right now that it only takes one person to make your life feel good or great or phenomenal. Look in the mirror … there's your answer: it's you.

It's said that people divide into three camps:

1. those who make things happen

2. those who watch things happen

3. those who don't have a clue what's happening.

Your Mind Makeover is all about being in camp one.

People who are happy, successful and fulfilled are people who are highly motivated. And motivation is movement, which we will look at in the next chapter.

chapter two

WHAT MOTIVATES YOU?

Motivation is movement; it is the drive, hunger, incentive, motive and push that creates and triggers action. It's that simple. Let's get one thing clear from the outset: nothing will ever happen for you until you feel motivated to get off your butt and take the necessary action that will move you towards your dreams and desires. Only then are you empowered to create lasting, positive change.

So decide right now to tap into your own enormous reserves of motivation and energise yourself to move forward towards what it is you want. My aim is to help you find the motivation to want to go for big dreams, visions and goals. There's no point, or gain, in aiming small in life.

> *Think big. You can't surf on*
> *a toothpick.*

So what motivates most people to take action? The answer is the two empowering emotions of inspiration and desperation. Both have a place in your life and have the capacity to generate high levels of motivation, as a consequence of which you will genuinely want to commit to taking massive action. As I touched upon in Chapter 1, inspiration and desperation are opposites, but each plays a vital role as a catalyst for action.

FEELING DISTURBED

I believe that if you want to create a great life you must first 'get disturbed' (this phrase was first coined by the famous American life coach Anthony Robbins). Feeling disturbed is a powerful emotion to use to your advantage – I certainly use it often. It propelled me to write this book, because when I imagined how I would feel if I did not write it, I felt so disturbed that I knew with absolute certainty that not writing the book was not an option. The result – massive movement, massive action and a book!

When you feel disturbed, you are empowered to instigate change and enrich your life. It moves you on to create positive shifts in your thinking, emotions, behaviour and actions. Simply said, you will move up a gear and take ownership of your life and the results you achieve.

Here's a motivating quote from the film *Hitch*:

> ❢ Your life is not measured by the number of breaths you take; your life is measured by the moments that take your breath away ❢

How does this quotation make you feel? Do you want to create and have new experiences that will take your breath away? Of course you do. Everyone does. Such questions often expose feelings of inspiration and desperation. But although the latter has negative connotations, as I've pointed out, it is not necessarily a bad thing and can be of great benefit to you. The key is to understand and accept that these two polar opposites play vital roles as motivators in your life – and use both to your advantage in order to achieve your goals.

USING DESPERATION AS MOTIVATION

Many of us would prefer to ignore the topic that follows but it's the one that's guaranteed to make us all experience a 'STOP and take a life check' moment.

Your mortality

You cannot control the length of your life but you can sure make a difference to its breadth and depth. When thinking about and facing their own mortality many people achieve the highest state of motivation possible and, as a result, take decisions and action way outside their comfort zones. They are fully committed to focus positively, think, plan and act with an energy surge they have never tapped into before.

But why do we need to face our own mortality to get to this immense level of motivation?

We each come into this world on our own and leave

it on our own, so we should take full responsibility for ourselves in between. Life is so very precious. If we truly acknowledged this, then each of us would grab our life with all the passion and intensity it deserves. We would strive to live every day of our lives with energy and commitment and make it the best life possible. We would take this gift of life and do whatever it is we want to do with it, right *now*. Death is the one thing none of us can avoid and nothing – not money, power, connections, intelligence, knowledge or action – can stop it. So let's begin now and live life with the vigour, passion and focus that it deserves.

I'm not referring to your mortality to make you feel sad. I'm asking you to think about it for one reason only, and that is to encourage you to tap into your highest possible level of motivation. I want you to take ownership of the precious life you've been given, right now, this minute and commit to living it to your full potential, every single day.

Perhaps if we all focused on our mortality regularly, even for just a brief moment, we wouldn't procrastinate and put things off. We would each live with an 'I'll do it now' attitude, versus 'I'll do it tomorrow' or an 'I should have; I could have' attitude. As the life coach Anthony Robbins says:

> *The road of 'someday…' leads to a place called Nowhere and you don't want to go there.*

It's your life and no one else can live it for you. Think about the following saying:

> *The sadness of life is not in 'having died'. No, the sadness of life is in* not *having lived while we are here and able to.*

The film *Out of Africa* is based upon the real-life story of Karen Blixen (played by Meryl Streep), who broke the boundaries of what everyone felt her life should be. When she was asked if she was frightened by going out alone into the African wilderness she replied, 'No, my only fear was that I would reach the end of my life and realise I had lived someone else's.'

Many people I have worked with have shared their personal experiences of desperation – for example at having missed an opportunity or not seized a career or life path they should have – and how it motivated them to change their expectations and their actions.

Here are the ones I've heard the most often:

- I will never miss an opportunity like that again in my life, career, relationships.

- I will never allow someone else to determine my own self-worth.

- I will not allow limiting beliefs to determine my levels of success.

- I will never have a relationship with a person who behaves that way towards me again in my life.

- I will never repeat that experience or that feeling again.

Do any of these experiences sound familiar to you?

Desperation can drive and power some of the greatest successes in life. Consider the many people who face enormous challenges, from losing someone very dear to them, to experiencing an abrupt end to a relationship or career, yet overcome their desperation to go on to achieve amazing results and live phenomenal lives. Whatever their experience, they use whatever happened to them and their desperation to motivate them to re-evaluate their lives. From challenge and adversity they make drastic and dramatic changes and go way outside their comfort zone. And the result? A positive outcome and a life moving forward.

Let me be clear here. It is not necessary for something desperate to happen in your life to put you into this state of peak motivation. You can create the immense motivation and get a phenomenal life for yourself in the precise moment you decide to!

OWN YOUR EXPERIENCES – NO MATTER HOW DIFFICULT

My strongest experience of desperation came when my wonderful dad passed away, at just sixty-four years old. He was my world and the shock of his death brought me to my knees and, to be honest, kept me there for a long time (no doubt he would have said, 'for goodness sake Sharron, get up; it'll play havoc with your knees'). Dad and I were similar in so many ways – we finished each other's sentences, shared ambitions, ideas, achievements, goals. Mum called us the Mutual Admiration Society. Simply put, Joe Lowe was my favourite person.

The grief was raw and I often felt great tidal waves of sadness engulf me. Yet ultimately there came a point when I had to stop and dig deep to find the motivation to take responsibility for how I was feeling and behaving. There and then I decided to live with the attitude that this was life as I knew it now and it was up to me to make the very best of it. I made the choice to strive for life as I wanted it to be, versus simply surviving it as it was. And of course that's what Dad would have wanted.

To help keep me focused and motivated, I wrote this down and stuck it onto the fridge door: 'If I plan to sit and wait for something or someone to turn up and make this feel better then I might as well start with my shirt sleeves, as they are about all I have that will "turn up" with this kind of negative thinking. I own my life and if I want a helping hand I'll use the one at the end of my arm.'

There was no doubt that at this point I needed a Mind Makeover. My feelings of desperation got me to move forward positively and I knew with absolute certainty that my attitude and thinking would allow me to survive and build a happy and fulfilled life. So how did I go about taking responsibility and moving forward? I used four 'pillars' of strength and support. I decided to:

1. Own it (my life)

2. Focus on the future (opportunities and possibilities)

3. Live with a positive energy (passion and enthusiasm)

4. Cultivate self-belief (confidence and determination)

As a direct result of taking ownership of my life – which essentially meant taking full responsibility for my feelings, actions and current situation – I was also able to find the courage to end a relationship that was emotionally, spiritually and financially draining. Most of us, male or female, can relate to this: it was one of those relationships where I felt as if I'd been running uphill to get to where I wanted to be with someone holding onto my shirt tails, pulling me backwards. When we move on from a relationship that drains our joy and personal growth it's a powerful life lesson that helps put us on the path towards getting our best life yet.

What then? My self-worth and confidence, which had been on the floor, returned and I felt as though an enormous weight had been lifted off my shoulders. I asked myself the question 'What is it I want to have, do and be in my life?' I made my life plan – a list of all the things I still wanted to do and achieve in my life (a 'bucket list' of sorts) – and followed it. I moved to London and seized and created lots of opportunities in both my business and social life.

At one point the family joke was that I would have gone to the opening of an envelope! But I ticked off experiences that I hadn't even imagined putting on my bucket list and my life evolved into a fabulous and fulfilling one, packed with new experiences and achievements.

So how would you like your life to be?

Your own bucket list

You will almost certainly have heard of the bucket list. Creating one is a great way to focus on what you want as it forces you to face the question: What do I want to experience, do and have in my life that I haven't yet? (And I'm not referring to material possessions here.) What would you put on your list?

EXERCISE

Put together your bucket list

The point of this isn't to think about what you'd do if you won the lottery – so one-year world cruises are out! Instead you need to think about how you would choose to live your life so that it really made a significant difference to you now. Think about the following:

- What changes would you make to your life as it is now?

- What job would you decide to do?

- Who would your friends be?

- What new experiences would you create and embrace?

- Who or what drains your positive energy that you would put a stop to?

- What new hobbies would you take up?

- What and who would make you laugh out loud?

- Who would you make amends with?

- Where would you travel to?

What are the most important things that you would put on your bucket list? What are your top five? Write them down.

Remember, you don't have to wait for something desperate to happen in your life, as I did, to get you into this state of peak motivation. You can create this level of motivation to get a phenomenal life for yourself in the exact same moment you make a decision to! Wouldn't NOW be the perfect time to begin?

Now let's look at the polar opposite of desperation, namely inspiration, and how it can provide you with the motivation to move your life forward.

USING INSPIRATION AS MOTIVATION

Feeling inspired is great. It's that feeling you get when you have achieved – or are about to achieve – something special, a major goal, or when you know you have done something exceptionally well. When you are in an inspired state you feel adrenaline, passion, enthusiasm … and you simply don't want that fabulous feeling to stop.

Use the motivation that this creates to empower you. As I pointed out in the Introduction, successful people and companies consistently increase their results and positive outcomes by focusing on what is positive, inspirational and wonderfully memorable. They focus on what inspires them to attract more of the same to them. As a consequence they feel an abundance of inspiration, passion, confidence and self-belief.

I hope you now feel there's no going back and you will be more aware of the things in your life that make you feel inspired or desperate, so you can use these highly motivating emotions to turn your life into the one you really want.

EXERCISE

Learning from your experiences

1. Write down three personal inspirational experiences and then ask yourself the following:

   ■ Why did these experiences motivate me to take action?

   ■ What results did I achieve?

   ■ What did I learn?

2. Write down three personal experiences of desperation and then ask yourself the following:

   ■ Why did these experiences motivate me to take action?

- What results did I achieve?

- What did I learn?

3. What impact did each of these six experiences have on me and my success?

Use the power of gratitude to get inspired

Gratitude is an incredibly valuable emotion for creating inspiration and motivation. If you are thinking that you have nothing to be grateful for, stop such thoughts now (and may I suggest that you take this book and hit yourself with it!). Think back to Chapter 1 and what I shared with you about Centrepoint.

For fifteen years I have been running Mind Makeover workshops for young women at Centrepoint, the London-based charity that supports and protects homeless people. Feeling inspired is not something that comes easily to many of the young women I meet there. For them, at a time in their lives when they should be at home being nurtured by family members who love them, they find themselves homeless and alone, until they reach Centrepoint and safety.

Obviously most of the women are only too familiar with feelings of desperation, so it's important for them to balance that by experiencing a positive emotion, like inspiration, that they can learn to use as a catalyst for positive change. How do I get them to feel inspired? I start by asking them, 'What are you grateful for?' Most of the young women just stare at me, obviously thinking I must be mad to ask such a thing and what on earth could they be grateful for. It's understandable; gratitude is an emotion that's rarely or never occurred to them because often they will have terrible past experiences, sleeping rough on the streets and living in fear.

But I do ask them this. Why? Because as their personal success coach it's my job to help them make positive shifts in their thinking so they can reframe how they see their lives and what they think is possible for them in the future. As I said in Chapter 1, to do this we must start with thinking about and focusing on what's right and not what's wrong.

A lot of my focus at the workshops is on the following statement:

> *If you do not like something then change it and if you cannot change it then change the way you feel about it.*

By the end of their Mind Makeover workshop, the resilient young women usually tell me that they now feel an emotion they have rarely or never felt before in their lives – gratitude! And, better still, they make a list of things they now feel grateful for. I imagine it's probably a very different list to the one you and I might complete, but the following examples from their lists should inspire you and make you feel very grateful for your own list:

- I now feel safe living at a Centrepoint project.

- I have people at Centrepoint who look out for my best interests and want to help me.

- I've been given great opportunities to learn new skills, get an education and they'll help me to apply for jobs.

- I've got new friends who are there for me. (These tight friendships are built upon a mutual appreciation of surviving an extremely tough youth.)

When you focus on what you feel grateful for and appreciate what you have in your life right now you will always have a life of plenty and you will attract more of what's good back to you. In other words, happiness, success and fulfilment kick in when you focus on appreciating what you have already. It's easy to think about what's wrong in our lives but it's also just as easy to think about what's right. Do not spoil what you have now by ignoring it and only desiring what you have not got yet. Take a moment to think about the things you now have in your life that were previously on your list of wishes and hopes for the future. So always focus on the good; on what you appreciate and are grateful for and you'll attract more good things back to you.

EXERCISE

What are you grateful for?

- Write down five things you can appreciate and be grateful for that are in your life right now. We're talking people, situations, feelings and opportunities ... not just possessions.

- What is it you appreciate about these five things?

- Now think of five things that you can appreciate and be grateful for about yourself as a person? (Think of your skills, knowledge, experiences and talents.)

- What is it you appreciate about these five things?

> *Appreciate what you have now and*
> *you will always have enough.*

IT'S PERSONAL

Personal success and fulfilment are just that, personal to you. Each of us has our own ideas of what happiness, success and fulfilment mean. One person's interpretation of success is not another's or we would all be going for the same jobs, driving the same model of car, travelling to the same destinations, dating the same type of person and enjoying the same hobbies.

If you decide right now that you want to take control of your personal happiness, success and fulfilment and that you will take massive action to move you from where you are now to where you want to be then that's tremendous and I'm delighted for you. But don't be mistaken: this is not a book simply to read for a quick fix. It is a 'take action' book, so you must act if you want the results you dream of. Otherwise you might as well buy two copies of this book and fasten one under each foot. Then at least you'd achieve one benefit – you'd walk a little taller!

But joking aside, as you know, life is not a spectator sport, it's a 'get off the sofa, go out onto the pitch and play it with all your heart' sport. One year from now, three years from now, a decade from now, know with absolute certainty that you will be far more disappointed by the things you did not do than by the things you did do. So, wouldn't now be a good time to start and take action? As always the choice is yours. Don't let anything hold you back from living true to your potential. Today will become tomorrow's yesterday so you've no time to lose.

In the next chapter I'll share some of the things that hold many people back from living their best life yet. I don't want anything to stop you.

chapter three

SUCCESS MYTHS AND COP-OUTS

Here's a question for you: would you fill a rucksack with heavy stones then put it on your back and carry it around with you all day? Of course you wouldn't – that would be ridiculous. There's no sense in doing this, just as there's no sense in carrying around the weight of success myths and cop-outs day in and day out. Yet many people do. They unconsciously carry them through their lives, like a heavy weight on their back that pulls them down, stopping them moving forward and achieving their goals.

Does this scenario apply to you? Think about the following myths and cop-outs: are they familiar to you?

SUCCESS MYTHS

First on the list is the myth that success and happiness are dictated by our genes or our environment.

MYTH 1

Some people are just born successful

Being a happy, successful and fulfilled person is not a gene given to one baby at birth and not to another. Imagine a maternity ward filled with newborn babies, all snug in a row of cots. There isn't a fairy godmother flying above the cots sprinkling fairy dust and success glitter over some of the babies and not over others.

And you certainly aren't placed in the delivery ward with a 'This is your life' tag on your toe saying one of the following:

- You'll have a happy life

- You'll be miserable and a moaner

- You'll have an average life

- Oh dear, you'll go through life blaming everyone else for all the things you haven't done or achieved, or

- Oh lucky you, you will have a phenomenal life.

There is no mystical force at work at the start of our lives giving one person a brilliant future and another person a lousy one. Happiness, success and fulfilment are states and emotions that we create and control. Your destiny is just that – *your* destiny. It's in your hands and you are in charge of the controls.

You are born positive, powerful and full of imagination and potential. Who you become is dependent upon:

- What you think about and focus on

- How you perceive and interpret what happens to you and what things mean to you

- What you do about it – the decisions and actions you take.

So understand right now that creating and living the life you want isn't dependent on a family gene or your circumstances (and certainly not on being born under the right star sign or sprinkled with fairy dust and success glitter at birth). Life doesn't work like that and it's a myth and cop-out to think it does.

It is true that we are each born into different environments, and some people are dealt a better deck of cards and more advantages at the start of their life than others. We each receive varying levels of love, education, financial and family support. Yet each person also has the potential to create the life they want.

We all know stories of people who have demonstrated resilience in the face of adversity and soar to achieve the life they want. These are individuals who break through the boundaries and social disadvantages that have held others back.

How does this happen to one person in a less advantaged environment and not to others who find themselves in a similar situation?

The answer is that successful people:

- make better decisions about what to focus on, think about and believe is possible

- commit to ambitious activity and take positive, massive action

- are proactive and not reactive to their environment and circumstances.

The last point is a very important one. Such people are proactive in their personal focus, the decisions they make and the actions they take. They interpret situations simply as experiences and do not judge them to be either good or bad. Positive experiences are to be embraced and repeated or learnt from and viewed as opportunities for personal growth. Negative experiences are not viewed as such: they are challenges to overcome and solve, not obstacles that stop them getting where they want to get to in their life. They do not allow them to dilute their life or put a stop to their dreams.

Bear in mind that there are also many examples of people born into tremendous privilege – wealth, the best education and family love and support – who squander their advantages or, worse still, throw their lives away to addiction and abuse, and die tragically young.

Whether we prosper in spite of our environment and circumstances (and I don't mean solely financially) or fail to do so despite being given every advantage, each of us constantly face the following questions:

- **What?** What does any particular situation mean to us?

- **How?** How do we interpret the situation? Positive or negative? Do we learn from it or are we damaged by it.

- **What do we do about it?** What action will we take, if any?

Think about the following statement:

> *How we all live our lives is determined*
> *not so much by what life brings to us as*
> *by the attitude we bring to life; and*
> *not so much by what happens to us*
> *as by the way our minds look at and*
> *interpret what's happened.*

I share this with the fabulous young women I meet at Centrepoint and they rise to this challenge time and time again, despite their tough circumstances.

There will be much more on this powerful topic in Chapter 4.

MYTH 2
Success is down to luck

The second myth some people carry with them through their lives is that successful people are simply lucky and in the right place at the right time.

This myth is often believed by those who are not living the life they want and who see success and happiness as something that falls easily and often into the hands of others. If you think like this, you could spend a lifetime waiting for happiness, success and fulfilment to fall into your lap accidentally. Alternatively, you can go out and make it happen. Being happy and successful is not down to being lucky and in the right place at the right time. (Unless of course you bought a winning lottery ticket, and even then we read that winning doesn't always bring happiness.)

There will be times in your life when you are exposed to opportunities. At these pivotal times you have a decision and a choice to make as to whether or not you seize the opportunity and work with all you have in order to get all you want.

Success is when opportunity is met with commitment and good old-fashioned graft. If you are presented with opportunities in your life and you decide not to take them, know with absolute certainty that someone else will grab them. Opportunities dropped will always be picked up by someone else. How does that make you feel? Motivated to seize every opportunity I hope.

EXERCISE

Opportunities seized and dropped

Take time to make this personal to you and think of some of the key opportunities you've been presented with in your life: in your work, relationships, travels, for example.

- Think of three opportunities you seized and the impact of each one.

- Think of three opportunities you let go and the impact of each one.

- How do you feel about the opportunities you dropped? (Inspiration or desperation?)

- Thinking about the one you dropped that had the biggest impact on you, ask yourself what not seizing this opportunity cost you? (I don't mean financially, I mean the cost to aspects of your life such as your self-worth, joy and experiences missed.)

- What have you learnt from this exercise and what would you do differently next time?

I hope that exercise has really got you thinking – great outcomes begin as thoughts, so keep doing this throughout your Mind Makeover. Reflect on things past (rewind and learn from your experiences) and also think of things to come (desires and goals). And bear in mind that opportunities seized will always multiply, if you have the right attitude and work at it.

I have used the following mnemonic for many years to emphasise precisely the role luck plays in your happiness, success and fulfilment. LUCKY = labour under conscious knowledge (you). In other words:

- **Labour** – work

- **Under** – with

- **Conscious** – awareness (be mindful and present in the moment)

- **Knowledge** – learnt skills and information

- **Y** is for YOU – own it and take massive personal action.

As many great sportspeople have said when they are called lucky or a natural after a famous win: 'I find the more I practise, the luckier I get.' The same point was made in a brilliant American TV commercial where a lady in her eighties stops a young man on the streets of New York and says: 'Excuse me son, can you tell me how I get to Carnegie Hall?' The young man smiles and replies, 'Certainly ma'am, you just need to practise lots!'

Your destiny is not a matter of luck, it's a matter of focus and action. The next time you hear someone who is happy, successful and fulfilled described as 'lucky', look closely and you will see an individual who is working hard to utilise all their skills and knowledge. They're creating and seizing opportunities, taking personal responsibility for their decisions and implementing the actions necessary to achieve their goals. Essentially they're working with all they have for all they want.

I was once told the only place success appears before work is in an English dictionary.

MYTH 3
I'm just unlucky

Even more life-diluting than the myth that success is down to luck is the perception some people hold that they only ever have bad luck. And that's the label they use to describe themselves – unlucky.

Last year I was out shopping in London with a friend when there was a sudden torrential downpour. It was as though the sky had been unzipped and a water tanker had burst above our heads. We managed to stop a taxi and as we jumped in my friend said, 'Oh thank you, that was so lucky.' Without turning around the driver mumbled,

'Luck, huh. The only luck I have in my life is bad luck and if I didn't have that then I wouldn't have any luck at all.' Another day, another opportunity to give someone, a complete stranger, a Mind Makeover! (I feel like a hairdresser sometimes: odd parallel for a life coach I know, but they must often meet people and think OMG that hairstyle is a disaster, and immediately want to help. That's how I feel when I meet someone with the wrong attitude.)

If you believe that the only luck you ever get in your life is bad luck and that you're in the wrong place at the wrong time most or all of the time, then, guess what, that is precisely what you'll get. (There's more on the power of self-fulfilling thoughts in Chapter 5.)

Even more worryingly, if you believe you are unlucky then you must also think that you have little or no control over your circumstances. As a result you may not be taking responsibility for your life and making it as you want it to be. This may sound harsh but it's important that you recognise that this may have simply become a habitual way of being and thinking for you. The good news is that you can stop doing this now by taking ownership of your life and dictating the path it takes. And as the saying goes: 'Don't believe the world owes you a living. The world owes you nothing. It was here first.'

So, I hope we can agree to squash the myths that some people are born successful, lucky or unlucky. The truth is that it is up to you, and *now* is the perfect time to have a Mind Makeover and place full responsibility for your life firmly back in your own hands.

Now let's address the issue of success cop-outs.

SUCCESS COP-OUTS

During many years as a success coach I've heard many cop-outs to achieving success. Let's start by examining the one I hear most frequently.

COP-OUT 1
I don't have time (or tick tock, tick tock)

If I had a pound for every time I've heard, 'Oh your success strategies and tips are brilliant, but I really don't have time to do them because of X...' When people tell me this I feel like knocking some sense into them but of course I realise this isn't exactly an effective way to build a working relationship. Instead I ask them the following questions, which I would now like to ask you:

- How many times each day do you think to yourself or say to others 'I just don't have enough time; there aren't enough hours in a day'?

- At the end of the day do you often think to yourself, 'I forgot to do/didn't get round to doing/should have done X, I didn't call Y or I forgot to email Z'?

- How many times do you go to bed at the end of the day and drift off thinking of all the things you didn't do, only to wake in the morning feeling overwhelmed by your to-do list for the day ahead?

Many people go through their day repeating that they don't have enough time like some sort of mantra, often with a hint of martyrdom in their tone (tip: if you relate to this, stop – other people soon find it boring). If you do this, even if it's self-talk (what you say when you talk to yourself), it will only increase the feeling that you absolutely do *not* have enough time. Believing this will make you feel anxious and frustrated and is one of the biggest triggers of stress, as it makes the day feel unsuccessful and unfulfilled and, in the longer term, makes you feel that your life is out of your control.

Do you relate to this? Am I describing you at times? Then let me ask you what I ask those who tell me they are always time-starved: what's your favourite TV programme? Who do you think should win *X Factor*? What's happening in *EastEnders* and *Coronation Street*?

When I ask these questions people can often tell me the plot in great detail. My next question is always, 'So exactly how many hours every week do you watch television?'

For most, and maybe for you, the answer to the question of how they use their time exposes precisely why they feel 'time starved'. It's always a light-bulb moment and for many it is the catalyst that gets them fired up to make positive changes and take charge of their most precious commodity – time.

We all have the exact same time each and every day of our life: 24 hours, 1440 minutes, 86,400 seconds. It's non-negotiable. So isn't it obvious that the difference between people who live happy, successful and fulfilled lives and those who do not is how each person decides to use – or misuse – their precious time. We each make decisions on the activities we fill our time with.

Think about this:

> *Is what you fill your time with making*
> *you as happy and as successful as*
> *you could be? Is how you use time*
> *giving you your best life yet?*

Ask yourself: 'Am I filling my time with life-enriching experiences that generate feelings of happiness, success and fulfilment or am I watching other people's lives acted out in TV soaps or in DVD box sets for hours each week?'

Time used or wasted?

Time is *never* the barrier to people getting what they say they want. Lack of time is merely an excuse and a cop-out. Discard it right now because it does not serve you well.

A few years ago I was hosting a business dinner in a hotel and at the end of day one of a two-day managers' training programme, one delegate, let's call her Helen, was late for the pre-dinner 'meet and drinks'. She arrived twenty minutes after everyone else and said with enthusiasm and gushing emotion, to all present, 'OMG I'm *so* sorry I'm late but it was just so gripping … Susan was sent home early from work because she was ill and found Steve in bed with Sadie and they were screaming and fighting. I was glued. I never ever miss an episode!'

Yes, you guessed it. Helen was living her life through a TV soap. As a coach I've heard a lot of excuses, yet even I was thinking 'What on earth is she doing?' That very same morning I'd asked the delegates to write down two areas of their lives in which they felt they were not achieving their potential and did not feel fulfilled – and what they felt was the reason for this. This is what Helen wrote:

1. 'I am not being given the promotion I deserve by my company and line manager or reaching my full career potential. I don't know why.' (Oh Helen, the mysteries of life; please, it's a no-brainer.)

2. 'I feel really out of shape and unhealthy because of all the travelling I have to do in my job and it's knocking my confidence.'

In both examples, Helen was subconsciously pointing a finger of blame elsewhere, in particular blaming the company she worked for.

Later that evening I asked Helen to think back to when she had arrived at the reception twenty minutes late and had passionately spoken to all who would listen about a TV soap. Did she feel she had sent out a message loud and clear to her colleagues and the management team that watching an episode of the TV soap was far more important to her than attending the event on time? I got her to think of her answers to the following questions and the feelings her answers evoked:

- 'What do you feel is the management team's and your colleagues' professional opinion of how you behaved tonight?'

- 'If you decided to put the same level of energy, focus and commitment you have for this TV soap into the two areas of your life where you feel you are not achieving your potential then what changes would you expect to experience?'

I encouraged her to stop, think and re-evaluate what she was doing. I suggested she stop pointing the finger of blame at everyone but herself and start to take owner-ship and responsibility for the decisions she made and the actions she took. Why? Because once she understood and could see the benefits of taking ownership, then she would easily and speedily make the positive changes to move towards what she wanted (promotion and fitness). I call self-benefits, 'What's In it For Me?' (WIIFM). I use this question to help people want to make positive change. Once they identify their potential personal gain, they are always happy to take the action required. (For more on this see Chapter 5.)

Helen had a choice to make. She could either continue to sit on the sofa watching her soaps or get off it and start exercising. Her company always booked her into four- or five-star hotels, most with gym facilities and swimming pools, so there was no excuse (but if they hadn't she could still have found a way to do it). Crucially, Helen came to this conclusion herself after accepting that she alone created her world.

Could she make positive changes? Yes. Did she want to make positive changes, achieve her goals and feel fulfilled? Yes. She immediately made massive changes in her thinking, her perceptions and took full responsibil-ity (a Mind Makeover can work its magic incredibly quickly). She made decisions about the life she wanted to live, both in her career and socially. Ownership and responsibility were now where they should be, fully back in her hands.

Two years on and following further coaching sessions Helen now holds a top sales position in the same company and she has experienced career promotion beyond her wildest dreams. She's also pretty good at running marathons!

Just like Helen, I want you to come to your own conclusions about the best way to act and behave in your life in order to achieve what you desire. How you act and what you do must ultimately be your decision. Only then will you create a high level of personal commitment and ownership, which will far outweigh me or anyone else telling you what to do. You always have a choice about what is important to you, the decisions you make and the actions you take. What makes some people happy, successful and fulfilled, and some not, is the decision to go after what is important to them, such as promotion and fitness for Helen. Then they focus all their energies upon getting it. It really is that simple.

My aim is to get you to change your perception of time, value it more and accept responsibility for how you use it because it is precious. As a result you'll see time as a friend to work with on the journey of life and not as the silent enemy conspiring against you. What matters in your life is not time itself but what you do with your time.

EXERCISE

Time used or wasted?

- What three activities do you do that enrich you and help create the life you want?

- What three activities do you do that waste your time and move you away from the life you want?

- What positive changes will you now make? Use your answers to motivate you to make positive changes, take control of your time and get excited by the prospect. Make positive changes now to how you value and use your time because it is your most precious commodity, it's your life.

Feeling overwhelmed?

Of course at some point in our lives we all struggle with conflicting demands on our time and feel overwhelmed. At such times I have a selection of coping mechanisms to call upon so that I can bin the feeling and quickly move on. You can too if you use the following tips.

Compare diaries

When you feel overwhelmed, stop and focus on someone who fits an inordinate amount of life into their days. At the moment I think of a great friend of mine who once introduced herself at a function by saying her name followed by 'I'm a serial entrepreneur'. The description fits her perfectly. She is involved in numerous successful businesses, her family is all-important, she loves to travel, she pioneers new initiatives and donates her time to charitable causes. I think of what her 'to-do' lists must look like and by comparison I immediately feel back in control of my own. It works for me, so try it and if you don't know someone like this think of someone you've read about and admire.

Focus on what's important

Write down a list of all the things that you think you need to do. Putting your thoughts on to paper or on to your computer task list is de-stressing and calming as it gives you a sense of order. Now divide your list into:

- what's essential and must be done today
- what's desirable and could be done today
- what's nice to do yet could be left for another time.

The next step is obvious; clear what's essential before you move on. Then if you don't get everything done in the day, the tasks left will not cause you to feel stressed as they are non-essential.

Effective or efficient?

Another helpful system of prioritising tasks is to classify them as efficient or effective:

> *When I am being* effective – *then I am doing the job right.*
>
> *When I'm being* efficient – *then I am doing the right job.*

Both are necessary but always go for efficient before effective! It's not enough to be busy. The question is, what are you busy doing? It's no use spending five hours tidying the office files if you run out of time to write a crucial sales report. This helps you to check that your time is focused on what's important and on what will move you towards what you want to achieve and not away from it. It's a quick and easy way of thinking and ticking off tasks and activities in order of priority.

What's the impact?

Here's another strategy that works for me when that to-do list is long. Ask yourself these questions:

- What is the impact of doing this now (high or low)?

- What is the impact of *not* doing this now?

There's your answer. Sometimes the impact of not doing something far outweighs the impact of doing it and moves you to prioritise and take the necessary action. It quickly sorts out your priorities for the time you have available and shows you where your energies are best used to get you to where you want to be.

Stop – breathe deeply and visualise a calming scene

When you feel overwhelmed and stressed, stop, sit in silence – even if it's only for a very short time – and breathe deeply to still your mind and body. Focus on your breathing. Breathe in to a count of four and out slowly to a count of four. You'll soon begin to feel less stressed and much calmer. Visualise a positive scene: see a picture in your mind of something that calms you easily and quickly. I see a beach I know and love. I've done this so many times that I get an immediate feeling of calmness. (It feels so real I sometimes find myself reaching for the suntan lotion.)

I have used this invaluable technique many times, but one occasion sticks in my mind. I was presenting at a global conference, giving three sessions to managers from three different country groups and I had to learn large amounts of specific data for each. On the day of the presentation to group A, I got up early to do a final rehearsal of this group's specific data. However, nine minutes before the presentation, I was informed that the groups had changed at the last minute and I would be presenting to a different group with different data.

Did it feel overwhelming? It certainly did. But there was a job to do and feeling overwhelmed wouldn't help me pull it off. I took a three-minute break and sat in silence, taking deep breaths, stilling my mind and positively focusing on the fact that I had previously prepared for all three presentations – and not just the one I had rehearsed early that morning. I did this with a mental picture of my perfect beach and I also visualised the presentation going really well. I stilled my mind and focused on a feeling of calmness. I returned to the conference room calm and smiling and thoroughly enjoyed giving my presentation. This technique got me into the right frame of mind to pull this off and demonstrates that although we cannot control all that happens to us we can control how we react.

To still your mind is to revitalise yourself.

COP-OUT 2
Procrastination: are you a doer or a gonna?

Ask yourself, are you a doer or a gonna? This expression comes from my father, who always said: 'There are two types of people in life, the gonnas and the doers.' The gonnas are always 'gonna' do something yet they never get around to it and usually blame everything and everyone else for it. They are full of excuses and nothing is ever their fault. I often say at conferences, 'If you're going to procrastinate, then procrastinate later!'

And then there are the doers. They are the opposite of the gonnas and they keep focused on what they want, continue to learn, grow, take action and make what they want happen. Doers take the action that is necessary so that what they want becomes what they have.

Decide right now to be a doer not a gonna in life.

COP-OUT 3
Blaming others

We've all heard of the blame culture. Don't become part of it – don't blame others for the things you want but don't yet have or the things you have not achieved. Take responsibility for yourself. It's beyond empowering when you do this as you are putting yourself firmly in the driving seat of your own life and not being a passenger along on someone else's ride. Don't look to anyone or anything else to create your life for you. Creating your best life yet is about taking responsibility for yourself and not waiting on others to do it for you.

I remind myself never to blame others by picturing what happens when we physically point the finger of blame at someone else. Think about it: there will be one finger pointing at them and three fingers pointing where? Yes, right back at lovely you, showing you that you should take three times more responsibility for your life, actions and achievements than you choose to park at the door of others or outside influences.

COP-OUT 4
I can't do it

In my coaching work people often say to me, in a voice full of emotion, 'I can't do it'. Mostly that's not what they actually feel or mean. After a short conversation we usually uncover that what they really mean (yet are not saying) is something like:

- I can't do it because *I don't know how to*

- *I can't be bothered* to do it

- I can't do it because *I don't want to.*

For example, when someone says any of the following: 'I want to learn a new skill or get a new career … but I can't because of X' or 'I want to get fit' or 'I want to save money … but I can't because of Y', they are selling themselves the line that it's not their fault or responsibility. This is not true and will give them absolutely nothing except a condition I call 'Excusitis' (excuse overload).

When you say the words 'I can't' you block your positive

energy, potential and personal growth. My role as your success coach is to help you to expose what may be preventing you from achieving the level of success you want. I want to get you to explore your thinking and perceptions so you come to your own conclusions as to the best way to progress with your life. I want to get you to accept the consequences of thinking or saying:

- 'I can't do it because *I don't know how to.*' Now you know what the block is you can unblock it with training, knowledge, practise and support.

- '*I can't be bothered* to do it.' Now the truth is out, connect to the benefits of doing it – think about WIIFY, or What's In It For You, and then use this motivation to take action.

- 'I can't do it because *I don't want to.*' If it's something you don't have to do then stop wasting your time and instead focus on what you *do* want to do. If it's something you don't want to do but must, at work for example, then you'll need to commit to doing it, do it well and then move on to what you want to do.

When you think 'I can't' you will not seize opportunities and will block positive energy coming to you. As I pointed out previously, someone else who does not suffer from excusitis will be right there to grab that opportunity. Their only difference is that they thought 'I can do it' and you thought 'I can't do it'. Remember, whether you think you can or whether you think you can't, you are right both times!

Talking to an audience – could you do it?

What if I asked you to give a presentation at a conference or a speech to a large group in a social setting? What would your reaction be? How would you feel? Around ninety out of a hundred people will immediately think 'I can't do that'.

This was precisely the reaction of one executive I worked with. I was asked to be his coach, as he had resisted any form of public speaking for months and it was adversely affecting his career. He told me exactly what he'd told his boss: 'I can't do that' (accompanied by a look of sheer horror). He didn't realise it at the time of course but what he meant was 'I don't know how to' not 'I can't do'.

For any of us, facing a task without the skill or knowledge to do it is daunting and not something I would recommend. Instead you need to acquire the necessary knowledge, training and skills to do the job well. Go and get what you need to excel at the job in hand and make it memorable (for all the right reasons!).

As the executive's success coach it was my job to dismiss 'I can't' by giving him the motivation to want to learn how to give a memorable presentation. I got him to focus on how he would feel once he conquered and achieved this. (He told me it would feel awesome and it would boost his confidence beyond words.)

I helped him realise that the only thing he had been missing in the past was the knowledge of *how* to do it. Remember the mnemonic 'LUCKY' from earlier in this chapter? Labour Under Conscious Knowledge? When you work with knowledge you'll achieve success, so fill that gap in your knowledge and you're moving. Your 'I can't' quickly becomes 'Yes I can'.

Also, when you decide to go after and achieve something you previously thought you could not do, I guarantee you will get back the very best feelings of fulfilment and personal pride. Your confidence and self-worth will soar.

So it's over to you. Whenever you hear yourself using the excuse 'I can't do it', *stop*. You now have the solution. Get rid of the condition of excusitis and replace it with the motivation you need to take action. You'll feel like a winner every time.

Focus on personal gain and you forget the pain

When I meet someone who insists 'I can't do it', but I know they really mean 'I can't be bothered' (a lethal cocktail of low motivation and laziness), I always think of the sort of person who joins an exclusive gym and hardly ever goes, but loves to impress people by telling them they're a member. And of course if you query their progress they'll probably tell you 'It's just not working for me, nothing's changed. It's the family genes. We're all really big boned...' (Watch out. Blame alert.)

If you're guilty of this, take heart – in my experience people (that's you and me) are never lazy. It's not how we're made. You simply need to get motivated enough, and once you identify what it is you really want to gain you forget any pain and go for it.

COP-OUT 5
Age and education

Do any of these statements sound familiar to you?

- 'I'm too old to do it'

- 'I'm too young to do it'

- 'I don't have enough experience'

- 'I didn't get a degree'

- 'I'm not qualified enough'

- 'I'm over qualified'

These are all related to good old 'excusitis'. Be careful, it's highly contagious. Get rid of it and change your thinking. Lack of self-belief is your only obstacle to getting what you want.

Here are some interesting facts:

- At seven years old Mozart published his first musical composition.

- At ninety-four years old George Bernard Shaw, the celebrated playwright, produced another award-winning show.

Should anyone ask you 'What's your best age?' always answer 'Right *now*'s my best age!' Think about this for a moment and realise that age is only a number – unless you allow it to become a label that restricts and stops you getting your best life yet. Don't let it.

Age has nothing to do with achieving your dreams when you compare it to passion and determination. Apply these two qualities to your life and age drops way down the list of the factors that influence your life.

Someone I once worked with had a huge upheaval in her personal life. It came out of the blue and rocked her secure world. She re-evaluated what she wanted from life and decided to leave her profession and retrain as a florist, a passion she had held since being a teenager. She told me her best friend was very concerned about her decision and said to her in horror, 'But you can't retrain at your age, you'll be fifty-two years old for goodness' sake when you finish training!' She told me she had calmly smiled at her friend and said, 'But don't you see, I'll get to being fifty-two years old whatever I do so I might as well be fifty-two and living my dream life as a florist.' And the winner is … the florist.

Just remember: it's never too late to become the person you want to be. At ninety-three years of age former engineer Clifford Dadson, from Cumbria, became The Open University's oldest graduate, gaining a BA Open Degree in Arts. His accomplishment came sixty years on from his last educational experience. Clifford hopes his achievement can serve as encouragement to others to fulfil their ambitions.

The flip of the coin is Sir Richard Branson, who struggled in school and dropped out aged sixteen – a decision that ultimately led to the creation of Virgin Records.

Age and education are not barriers to living your best life yet unless you see them as such.

EXERCISE

Your personal cop-outs

Think of the excuses you have used and write down your answers to the following questions:

- What cop-outs have you used in your life?

- What impact has this had on you?

- What will you do differently in the future?

UNLOCK YOUR POTENTIAL

Success myths and cop-outs disappear when you commit to your own Mind Makeover, with the result that:

- Perceptions become realities.

- Problems become opportunities.

- Negative focus becomes positive energy.

- 'I can't' becomes 'I can'.

- Fear of taking action becomes faith in taking action.

- New goals are imagined, and *not* goal planning is not an option.

- Desire and self-belief hit a new high.

You now know the success myths and cop-outs that consciously or subconsciously may be holding you back from unlocking your potential, taking action and living your best life yet. Make sure you throw them out of your life. NOW.

Let me ask you a question. What separates people who lead happy, successful and fulfilled lives from those who live dissatisfied and unfulfilled lives? The answer to this vital question will tell you all you need to know to achieve all you desire. It is the key to unlocking all you want to have, be and do.

Successful people know the answer to the question and use it: it unlocks their potential and helps them get the best out of each and every day. Whether their goals and dreams are focused on their career, relationships, finances or physical and spiritual well-being, or all of these things, they each share one very powerful common denominator. What is it? You will find the answer in the next chapter.

chapter four

THE PHENOMENAL POWER OF YOUR MIND

In my role as a success coach the questions I'm asked the most, whether by senior executives and managing directors or in social situations, are the following:

- What's the one common denominator of all successful people?

- Why are some people happy while others are miserable?

- What's the one sure thing that guarantees success?

- What separates high achievers from non-achievers?

The questions – and the people asking them – may differ but the answer being sought is the same one. Executives and managing directors ask because the answer unlocks the secret to developing a company's greatest asset, namely its people, and generating phenomenal growth.

In social situations people ask the question because they want to experience success, or more of it. For you, the answer to these four vital questions is the key to unlocking your potential and realising all you want to be, to do and to have.

THE CHARACTERISTIC THAT UNDERPINS SUCCESS

So what is the one common denominator of everyone who leads a happy, successful and fulfilled life? In order to answer that let me quickly take you through a powerful exercise that I used recently with an audience of over twelve hundred delegates at a company conference. I asked the delegates to write down the answer to the most common question that I'm asked:

> *What is the one 100 per cent common denominator of all happy, successful and fulfilled people?*

Here are the top ten answers given by the delegates, in order of popularity:

1. Knowledge

2. Hard work

3. Goal planning

4. Leadership

5. Time management

6. Resilience

7. Ownership

8. Focus

9. Passion

10. Commitment

When you look at this list, is it similar to the list you would write yourself or is anything missing? Which would you choose as your answer? Is your answer even on this list?

To illustrate the correct answer I used the following word game – it's a great way of embedding the answer in your mind.

A	=	1	J	=	10	S	=	19
B	=	2	K	=	11	T	=	20
C	=	3	L	=	12	U	=	21
D	=	4	M	=	13	V	=	22
E	=	5	N	=	14	W	=	23
F	=	6	O	=	15	X	=	24
G	=	7	P	=	16	Y	=	25
H	=	8	Q	=	17	Z	=	26
I	=	9	R	=	18			

Take a look at the chart above, starting with the alphabet. You can see it runs from A–Z in alphabetical order. Now look at the numbers, which run from 1–26, in chronological order and following precisely the same order of A–Z. There are no gimmicks. We're going to take the two most popular answers from the delegates' list and spell them out using the corresponding numbers from the alphabet table. What we're looking for is a score of 100, which will give us the answer – the 100 per cent common denominator of all happy, successful and fulfilled people.

OK, let's play the word game. Here is the word that more of the twelve hundred people chose than any other. The answer to the question for them was 'Knowledge'. Let's add it up according to the chart to see if it gives us our '100 per cent' answer.

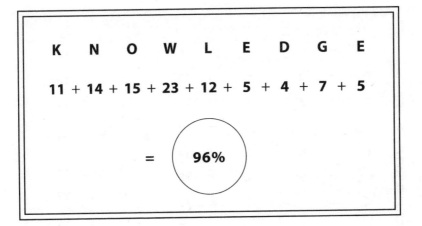

Knowledge scores 96 per cent so it is very important to achieving success, but I have met hundreds of people in life who are knowledgeable yet they definitely could *not* be described as happy, successful and fulfilled.

Why? Because they:

- have knowledge but do not share that knowledge with others; or

- share their knowledge but lack commitment and enthusiasm; or

- are bored by what they know and what they do.

Knowledge has no power without action. I recently spoke to a top media executive who said his team all had first-class degrees and the necessary knowledge but because none of them possessed a raw passion for their job they lacked energy and drive. Irrespective of your qualifications, if you lack passion your success will be limited. Knowledge without passion is like winking at someone you like in the dark. Result – nothing.

Let's look at another of the audience's answers, which was second on the list. Is hard work the correct answer, the magical 100 per cent?

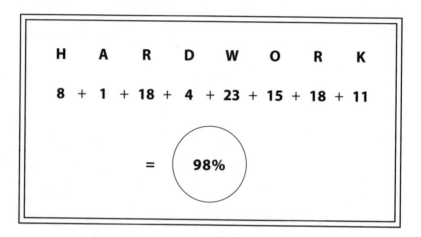

Nope, hard work is not the answer either. It adds up to only 98 per cent. Of course it's important to work hard, but there are many people who feel that they work incredibly hard yet the success and fulfilment they deserve still elude them. Maybe you know someone like this (maybe you are that someone!).

OK, I'll put you out of your misery.

THE ANSWER IS...

Number nine on the delegates' list was the word 'passion'. It's an ambiguous concept and open to many interpretations. I suggested another word. I replaced 'passion' with the word 'attitude': in fact I displayed it in massive letters on a 10-metre^2 screen. Why? Because attitude – or to be more precise the *right* attitude – is 100 per cent the common denominator of each and every person who lives a happy, successful and fulfilled life.

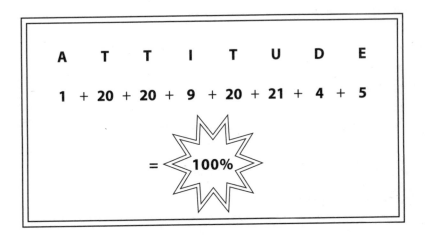

Yes, it adds up. Your attitude dictates 100 per cent your level of success, happiness and fulfilment.

But, wait a minute; it is also crucial that you know without doubt that attitude can also be 100 per cent the cause of your misery, frustrations and disappointments. That's the immense power of your own attitude. It can make you successful, if you decide to take charge of it, and it can also stop you being successful – if you don't!

Your attitude will give you:

- success as easily as failure

- happiness as easily as sadness

- faith as easily as fear

- inspiration as easily as desperation.

The phenomenal power of attitude has been understood for a long time. Knowing that your life is a reflection of your attitude isn't new. It's been said many times before:

- 'There is nothing either good or bad, but thinking makes it so.' *Hamlet*, William Shakespeare.

- 'Everything is possible for him who believes.' Mark 9:23, Bible.

- 'We are what we think. All that we are arises with our thoughts. With our thoughts we create our world.' Buddha.

Your attitude is yours and yours alone. Never doubt that it can be your secret weapon and your greatest supporter. When you know how to make your attitude work for you, then and only then will it give you all you desire.

> *It is your attitude (how you think) rather than your aptitude (what you know) that will determine your altitude in life (how high you fly).*

With your thoughts you create your world. So give yourself a Mind Makeover: start right now. I want you to know with absolute certainty that you are fully in charge of your mind. Success is an inside job and when you control your thoughts you control your world. Success grows quickly when you feed it with determination, commitment, tenacity, persistence, skill, strategy and knowledge. Add ambitious activity, namely action, and you'll be flying high.

If you doubt that this applies to you, it may help to consider one of my favourite fables about success. The story goes that far back in time the leaders of the world became very concerned that people were becoming clever, knowledgeable and successful too easily, so they decided to hide the secret of success somewhere so safe that it would never be found. They considered hiding it deep in the ocean, but decided that one day people would find a way to explore the ocean depths and would find it. They thought about hiding it on another planet but rejected that idea because people were bound to reach the stars one day too. Finally, they found the solution. They decided they would hide the secret of success in a place where people would never ever dream of looking for it: in their mind, attitudes and thoughts. It would be the very last place people would think to look for the secret of success.

My experience tells me that holds true for many, whether in business or generally in life. The mind, for many people, is still the last port of call in the search for success and happiness. Is it somewhere you have overlooked too?

EXERCISE

What's your starting point?

■ Do you consciously use your mind to control your thoughts and direct your actions towards what you want in life? Score yourself from 1 to 5: a score of 1 = I never do... and 5 = I always do... :

- Write down your score.

- What impact does your score have on your well-being?

- How do you think you will benefit from achieving a top score of 5?

When you score that magical 5 you will be using your mind to control your thoughts and happiness, and success and fulfilment will be yours.

GETTING THE RIGHT ATTITUDE

By now I hope you agree that the right attitude is the key to unlocking all that you want to have, to be and to do in life. At this point I'd like you to think about the following question, which I've asked of thousands of people during Mind Makeover coaching sessions:

> *How, when and where are you supposed to learn this vital life strategy?*

This question is usually met with puzzled looks and silence. Why? Very few people have ever been taught how to use their minds for maximum personal benefit so they don't know how to answer or where to start.

We're certainly not given this vital knowledge at birth by our fairy godmother sprinkling magic dust over us. And for most it isn't imparted at school or in further education. You may remember years of maths, science and English lessons but I bet you can't remember any lessons on the subject of 'Success' or 'How to achieve a happy, successful and fulfilled life by tapping into the immense power of the mind'. Me neither, but I do remember five long years of cookery classes, which I was unbelievably bad at. Can you imagine if all those hours of lessons had been used to educate and equip me with the knowledge of how to use my mind and attitude? I could have discovered a lot sooner where my true passions and interests were. Certainly not in cookery. To this day my heart sinks at the word 'bake'. The very best thing I can make for dinner is a reservation.

Ninety-nine per cent of the people I have coached felt that they lacked any real awareness or understanding of the power of attitude until the day they attended a Mind Makeover session. Deep down, subconsciously maybe, many may have known the answer is attitude. It is, after all, common sense, but it is not common practice.

So, to go back to my earlier question, how do you learn to develop and mould your attitude towards achieving success? Most of us will already have very set ideas and patterns of behaviour taken from our own experiences and emotions as well as through observing others, such as parents, teachers and peers, and then either mirroring their behaviours or acting against them. As a consequence, ways of being and acting become habitual and our personalities and behaviours are formed. The great news is that no habits are ever set in stone; all habitual ways can be changed and improved (and the ones we love can get even better). The first step in improving your attitude is to examine how it works and the immense impact it has on you and your life.

Let's see how well your attitude is serving you right now.

QUIZ: Test your attitude

Below you will find ten sets of statements on a particular aspect of attitude. Each set comprises two choices. In your notebook, write down whether you agree with statement A or B (so 1B, 2A, etc.) and at the end add up your score.

1.

A People just have to accept me as I am and what you see is what you get.

B I adjust my attitude to match the person I'm with and the situation I'm in.

2.

A I always have a choice about my attitude and behaviour.

B My attitude is fixed and was formed years ago. It's too late to change.

3.

A If I change my attitude I can bring about changes in other people and circumstances.

B People and things will be as they are going to be whatever I do.

4.

A My feelings and attitudes are what they are, and are out of my control.

B I fully control my attitude and what happens to me.

5.

A My attitude is a major factor in my success and
happiness.

B My attitude is a minor factor in my success and
happiness.

6.

A I believe other people are the main cause of my
problems.

B I believe I cause my own problems (and I'm
responsible for the solution).

7.

A My attitude and characteristics were fixed from an
early age.

B My attitude and characteristics will change and evolve
throughout my life.

8.

A I can grow from failure.

B When I fail there is no gain.

9.

A I live in the day and let my future happen.

B I consciously plan my future in advance.

10.

A My thoughts come out in all I do and say.

B My thoughts are private and hidden from others.

Score sheet

Answer	Points	Answer	Points
1 A	0	1 B	1
2 A	1	2 B	0
3 A	1	3 B	0
4 A	0	4 B	1
5 A	1	5 B	0
6 A	0	6 B	1
7 A	0	7 B	1
8 A	1	8 B	0
9 A	0	9 B	1
10 A	1	10 B	0

What the scores indicate

8–10 You have a positive attitude and are conscious of how your attitude affects the outcome and therefore your happiness and success. *The Mind Makeover* will help you further improve your positive approach to life.

5–7 At times you are aware of the role and power of your attitude. Aim to develop a consistent, positive attitude.

5 or less You will benefit from questioning your thoughts on the impact of your attitude upon your happiness and success.

Whatever your score; there is always room for improvement. Is your current attitude giving you your best life yet? Keep reading and trust me it will!

> *The biggest room in the world is*
> *the room for improvement.*

HOW ATTITUDE WORKS – THE ICEBERG THEORY

One of the simplest and most effective ways of understanding how attitudes work is to use the analogy of an iceberg (yes an iceberg). That may sound strange but I have shared the iceberg theory for over twenty-five years with thousands of people and I get great feedback about how incredibly useful people find it. So how does it work?

Look at the picture of the iceberg overleaf. Your mind is represented by the part of the iceberg below the surface: this is where you store your beliefs, experiences, motives and emotions (what you think). This part is huge in comparison to the tip of the iceberg, which represents your actions and behaviour (what you do). If you were in a ship alongside such an iceberg, the tip of it would look enormous, yet the reality is that you would only be seeing an eighth of it – seven-eighths are hidden from sight. There is a disparity in the size of the two parts of the iceberg but they are inseparable, interdependent and forever joined together (they are, in fact, one).

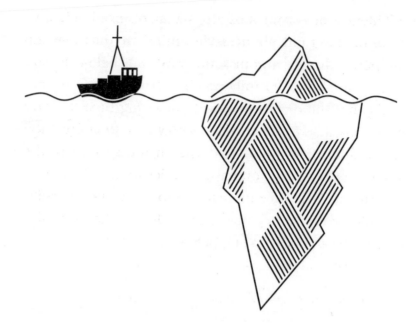

The point is that our thoughts control our emotions and attitudes and they, in turn, trigger our actions. The key here is that it works from the bottom up not the top down. Use this knowledge to give yourself an advantage in life. The part of the iceberg above the water is the only part visible to others. It is the visual representation of you and reflects all of your behaviours and actions. It is the part of you that others can actually see when they are with you and is the part of you that others judge you on. What you do, how you behave, what you say, how you say it, your voice tone, how you move and how you look, your body language – all of these things are visible for others to see.

So what is the driving force behind the one-eighth of the iceberg, the visible part? What power drives your actions, your behaviour, what you say, how you say it and how you look?

The answer is your attitude. What you predominantly focus on and think about in your mind are the force and the power that drive your actions. What is below the surface (your thoughts) fully powers what is above the surface (what you do). It goes without saying then that you must look at, understand and know how to control the part hidden from view 'underneath the surface of the water'. It's here that you have a choice to make and it's a critical one. Will you choose to live your life with a positive attitude or with a negative one? Will you choose to live your life as an optimist or a pessimist?

It's a critical choice because it will give you:

- attitudes that are either positive or negative

- thoughts that are either life enhancing or diluting

- perceptions that are either good or bad

- beliefs that are either limiting or bursting with imagination

- experiences that you view either as failures or lessons learnt

- self-worth that is either strong or weak

- self-talk that is either your friend or your enemy

- a focus on what is either possible or impossible

- moods that have either happy or sad emotions

- motives that are either sound or unsound.

The way you choose to see your world creates precisely the world you see. The good news is that with just a few small adjustments to your thinking, you can make a dramatic difference to how you feel and how you live your life.

You always have a choice. Choose a positive attitude to life and all things fall into place.

> *Nothing will stop the person with the right attitude and nothing will help the person with the wrong one.*

At this point you may be thinking 'Yes but no one can see my attitude … No one can see into this vast, hidden part of me where I keep my thoughts, dreams, worries, opinions, experiences, motives and feelings.' Well, yes they can and yes they do!

I spend my life reading other people's attitudes and, believe me, how they behave is a true reflection of their attitude and precisely what they are thinking. When you truly observe another person you can tell by their body language and their tone whether what they are saying and how they are feeling are in harmony with each other.

Say what you mean and mean what you say

Think about this. When you are talking to people do you often realise that what they are saying does not match with how they look or come across? Imagine someone saying very loudly 'I'm not angry' as a vein throbs in their neck. Or a waiter taking your order in a restaurant and, all the time they're asking politely if everyone has made up their mind yet, their pained expression screams out that they're bored and desperate to finish for the night. People do not always mean what they say or say what they mean. For example, I was in a meeting recently when someone said, 'Hold on a minute, I know you think you've just understood what I said but I'm not sure you realise that what you heard is not what I meant.' (Work that one out!) I'm sure you would agree that more people communicate in a confusing, ineffective way than in a clear, concise, effective way. Which camp are you in?

How you communicate is vital to your success. All communication begins in your mind and with your thoughts. Every action starts life as a thought and while that may not be visible – like the submerged part of the iceberg – each and every one of your actions and behaviours is 'above the surface'; it's out there for others to see. They are all driven by what is happening under the surface where the true power house lies, in your mind and your thoughts.

Before anything happens in the external world it must first happen in your internal world. All things begin as a thought and your thoughts will materialise into your world. In other words, what happens to you has less impact than what happens *within* you.

What you can see in the tip of the iceberg

The tip of the iceberg, that one-eighth of you that others can see, is broken down into three key areas:

1. your words

2. the tone of your voice

3. your body language.

Can you relate to the following statistics from your own experience? Think of your day-to-day communication and you will probably find that:

- your words (what you say) account for around 7 per cent of your impact

- your tone (how you say it, i.e. volume, rate, pitch) accounts for around 38 per cent of your impact

- how you look, act and move (your body language, i.e. facial expressions, hand gestures, posture) accounts for around 55 per cent of your impact.

We communicate with so much more than mere words. You and I also communicate through our attitude, which reveals our underlying emotions, motives, experiences and feelings. This is particularly true when we like or dislike something: in these instances our positive and negative thoughts are far more obvious in what we say and do than we realise. It's a fact that people will evaluate most of the emotional content of your message, not so much by what you say but by your nonverbal signals (what's going on in your head).

What you say

Your words are miniscule in comparison to what you think. This figure of 7 per cent is the approximate impact you have when you communicate with someone, whether that is in a business, social or family situation. This is how you are judged either consciously or subconsciously by others. Think back to the 'I'm not angry/throbbing vein' scenario and you'll appreciate how accurate this is.

Our words have the smallest impact and yet this is often where we put most of our attention, focus, preparation and planning, whether you are about to make a presentation, give someone some news or attend an important meeting.

How you say it

How you say something accounts for around 38 per cent of your impact. Saying 'How are you?' to someone you love and who is having a tough time will sound completely different to when you say 'How are you?' to a business colleague you are meeting for the first time. The intonation of your voice reflects your thoughts and attitude at the time you say it.

If you doubt that think about when a salesperson serving you in a shop says 'Can I help you?' in a sharp, frustrated voice and with an annoyed expression (because they are just about to go to lunch). Do you hear 'Can I help you?' Or do you hear the hidden thought of 'Will you please go away now?' The actual words become completely lost and insignificant.

Your body language

The impression you give and the impact you make is mostly driven by your body language and attitude. This, along with the tone of your voice, makes up around 93 per cent of the total impression you make.

Let's go back to the example of someone who is thinking angry thoughts yet saying something very different. They say to you, 'I'm not angry!' while shouting with their arms folded and their face up close to yours. The words (7 per cent) 'I'm not angry' are contradicted by the angry intonation (38 per cent) and angry body language (55 per cent). Their words do not align with how they look and sound. As a consequence, the words 'I'm not angry!' become completely lost. So watch out: what you do (how you look and sound) can shout so loud that others cannot hear the actual words you're saying. Tell yourself, 'If I think it, they'll see it because what's going on inside will show on the outside.'

Key question: can you see attitude?

Answer: damn right you can – never doubt it! If you want a demonstration of attitude in all its glory, think back to that famous clip from the film *Pretty Woman*, when Julia Roberts goes shopping on Rodeo Drive in LA. On her first visit the snooty sales people make her feel so uncomfortable that she quickly leaves the shop. However, after support from Richard Gere – and a head-to-toe designer outfit – she returns overflowing with designer shopping bags and says, 'Do you remember me? You wouldn't serve me yesterday. Are you on commission?' She then lifts all the designer carrier bags into the air and says, 'Big mistake, huge.' It's a fabulous scene.

Your attitude comes out in every single thing you say and do. We often talk more about a person's attitude when it is perceived to be a negative attitude, for example:

- 'She'll never get that promotion because she's got a terrible attitude'

- 'I returned the dress to the shop but the sales assistant was rude and had an appalling attitude'

- 'He's got such a negative attitude, it'll never work out'.

How often do you hear attitude being spoken about in a positive way, as below? Not so often, I would suggest.

- 'He's got a phenomenal attitude'

- 'She's got such a positive attitude, she lights up a room'

- 'She's got a magnetic attitude and just keeps attracting success and good things to her'.

THE ICEBERG THEORY IN PRACTICE

So let's cut to the chase here. Answer this pivotal question:

Do you think your personal attitude brings you emotions of happiness, joy and fulfilment:

- Always? • Often? • Occasionally?
- Rarely? • Never?

Has your answer motivated you to want to make positive changes to your attitude, moods and emotions? Let's look at one of the most practical and enjoyable ways to do that.

THE POWER OF COMPLIMENTS

A very good way to engender a positive attitude, both in yourself and in others, is the use of compliments. You will be amazed at the massive impact genuine compliments can have on a person's attitude and well-being. I continually tell people they are brilliant at what they do (obviously only when they really are). I believe that compliments are fabulous things to give and receive and you shouldn't miss opportunities to give them wherever and whenever you can. You will immediately make your days happier and brighter.

Giving other people compliments is something we can all do but do you compliment yourself? Now that's something many people struggle with.

Compliment yourself

The most important opinion is the one you have of yourself and the most significant things you say in your day are the things you think and say to yourself. So think about this: do you compliment yourself? When I ask people if they compliment themselves it often elicits a confused look because it's never occurred to them to do this. They will happily berate and complain about themselves but compliments, now that's a different thing altogether!

Don't get me wrong. I'm not suggesting you go through your day saying 'thank you' to yourself every few minutes, just that you take every opportunity to increase your own feel-good factor by giving yourself a compliment. You can either think it to yourself or say it out loud. If you don't already do this, don't judge it until you've tried it. Decide that just for today you will give yourself compliments at every opportunity. Then at the end of the day, ask yourself, 'Do I feel better?' (I guarantee you will do.)

Instead of looking in the mirror in the morning and saying things like, 'OMG I look awful today' or 'I've aged ten years overnight, those lines weren't there yesterday' or 'I've put so much weight on I've got to move that mirror' (not the best solution), say to yourself (with a smile) 'Good morning gorgeous!' or 'Good morning you handsome devil'. Do the same with how you look and feel. Don't say, 'I'm too fat or too thin', say, 'I'm great just as I am' (when you like and love yourself then you're happy to improve and polish your current version of yourself). If something doesn't go to plan, don't say 'I'm so stupid. What an idiot I've been.' Instead say, 'Yes I have made a mistake and it's a good thing because I'll learn from it and won't do it that way again.' Make it a habit to like and respect yourself – go on try it, compliment yourself because not only does it make you feel great; it maintains and builds your self-belief and confidence and that is an on-going process.

QUIZ: Compliments or complaints – which do you use most often?

Copy the following lists into your notebook and ask yourself the following questions (put a tick or cross in the appropriate column).

Do you compliment your...?

	Never	Rarely	Occasionally	Often	Always
Self	✓				
Best friend				✓	
Partner					
Close family					
Work colleagues					

Do you complain to your...?

	Never	Rarely	Occasionally	Often	Always
Self					
Best friend					
Partner					
Close family					
Work colleagues					

This quiz highlights the areas you need to change. You should be your own best friend and compliment yourself often. If you are more prone to complaining to yourself the following exercise will highlight this and help you turn it around.

EXERCISE

Choose compliments over complaints

I want you to get rid of any complaints you've been berating yourself with. If you decide to hammer yourself with complaints you will find many more things to complain about. It will gain a momentum and become a very bad habit. Delete each one from your mind or turn each criticism into a compliment. Think back over the last seven days and write down some of the things you've thought and said to yourself:

■ Write down five examples of when you were critical of yourself (diluting your happiness and success)

■ Now write down five compliments you gave to yourself (that increased your happiness, success and feel-good emotions). If you can't think of any then try to turn around the criticisms above. For example, turn 'my body looks like it needs ironing' (think about that!) into 'I appreciate my body for all the wonderful things it does for me and I now have the motivation to become fitter, healthier, happier and as a result feel in control.'

A compliment is simply an act of positive recognition. Genuine, substantiated compliments have a powerful impact on your attitude and well-being. For example: compliment yourself with 'I did great at work today, I got all my priorities ticked off (reason) and I enjoyed myself; I feel I've really achieved a lot (benefit).' When you shower yourself with compliments you will find many more things to be positive about. It gains a momentum and becomes a good habit absolutely worth cultivating.

The exercise I'm going to ask you to do next can have a big impact and help you to fast track to a more positive outlook.

EXERCISE

Describe yourself

You have **10 minutes** to do this (if you spend any more time on it than that, reality leaves and perception kicks in).

Write down anything that you feel describes:

- **How you look** For example, tall, short, fit (according to my niece, this now means something very different to its original meaning!), healthy, unhealthy, young, old, fabulous, OK, gorgeous, exhausted...

- **How you act** For example, grumpy, kind, smiley, critical, frustrated, angry, passionate, apathetic, happy, sad...

- **Your characteristics and values** For example, determined, worrier, risk taker, cautious, fearful, courageous, patient, impatient, organised, messy, passive, assertive, kind, honest...

- **Your skills and knowledge** For example, high, low, quick to learn, slow to pick up new things, great presenter, lousy cook...

- **Your attitude** Positive, negative, optimist, pessimist, glass half full or half empty...

OK, so look at your list and put a tick against everything that's a compliment (a friend). Now put an 'X' against anything that's a complaint (the enemy). This highlights whether you are your own best friend or your biggest enemy. Once you've highlighted the areas to change it becomes quick and easy to always be your own best friend. Remember, with complaints, either bin and delete them or change them by turning them into something positive and life affirming.

TAKE TIME TO CHECK PEOPLE OUT

Whenever I meet someone, irrespective of the circumstances, I always observe what I call their fullness. I don't mean their dress or suit size here, but their full impact. Yes, I listen to what they say, but I am far more interested in how they sound, look and act.

It is far more empowering and realistic to connect with a person's attitude (their thinking and focus) rather than merely concentrating on what they say and acting upon this. What someone says represents only a part of the picture you need. To get the most out of all your communication and interaction you need to delve into what the person 'feels' about what they are saying.

For example, if someone says to you when you ask how they are, 'I'm good thanks', yet, they look thoroughly miserable, avoid eye contact with you and have a voice tone bursting to the seams with boredom and apathy, it's obvious that they don't really feel 'good thanks'.

In my role as a success coach I have to probe and ask relevant questions so I can become fully aware and understand what is truly going on with my clients. A couple of useful tips I always follow, which you can apply at work or socially, are:

- don't expect results if you don't inspect your actions and the actions of others, yet

- know when to stop as too much analysis gives paralysis.

Now you are aware of the iceberg theory you know now that a person's actions and behaviour are a direct reflection of what they are thinking and feeling, so work with this information and knowledge to empower you. You'll communicate effectively and efficiently and see immediate results.

How to read other people

In any face-to-face communication you can now use your knowledge of the iceberg theory to go beyond basing your style of communication simply on what someone tells you. You can now delve much further into the other person's attitude and thinking by observing their voice tone and body language.

You should now be able to use the iceberg theory to communicate skilfully on two levels:

- above the surface (actions); and

- below the surface (attitude).

To do this you need to truly observe the full communication. Notice if their body language is relaxed, confident or unsure? Is their eye contact strong or are they looking away or at the floor? Is their handshake firm or weak? Is their voice tone confident or hesitant? Practise observing the full meaning of how others are communicating with you for even a short time and you'll soon get a feel of whether what they are saying and what they are feeling are in harmony.

What if it isn't in harmony and their words and actions clash? Don't accept the mere words. Continue by asking a question in a relaxed and confident manner to probe for more information. Probe to expose their feelings and real meaning. I often say something like 'I'd like to understand how you really feel about this' or 'I'm concerned that you may not be fully OK with what you're telling me'. Both show care and a concern to understand and collaborate with the other person. Because the communication is genuine and based on a sincere concern and desire to understand how the other person feels, in almost every situation I find the person is happy to open up and share their feelings and truths with me. Try this and you'll communicate effectively and efficiently and see immediate results.

On the telephone

Even when you are chatting to someone on the tele-phone, although you cannot see the other person you now have the knowledge and ability to connect deeply to the intonation of their voice and assess whether their tone matches the words. As a general rule, as you cannot see their body language (unless you are on Skype), then the effect of their tone increases and can have an impact as high as 90 per cent on the communication. So listen intently and absorb and assimilate their tone, pitch, speed and interest (or boredom).

Emails and letters

You probably spend a lot of your time communicating this way with people you can neither see nor hear. You may never meet or even speak to some of them. Be aware; the written word reflects the attitude of the person writing it. So check your attitude (positive, negative, frustrated, calm, angry?). Read it again before you press send. It sounds obvious yet it is often overlooked: how many of us have emailed or written and posted a letter that we wish we had read again first!

One of my clients holds a head office 'No-Email Day' four times a year, because they noticed that colleagues who sat right next to one another or perhaps within a few metres often didn't speak to each other for days on end yet they sent hundreds of one-liner emails to these same people. The managing director believed that people needed to reconnect with people.

What happens on 'No-Email Day'? If you think everything goes wrong you are mistaken. Because on these specific days, people have to get up and walk, talk, connect, reconnect, share information, empathise and communicate with each other face to face. As a consequence, these days have a positive ripple effect, creating better teams, synergy, co-operation and lots of fun and enjoyment. Of course emails have their rightful place in business and social life but this one idea got the team spirit back and made sure people talked as well as typed. Feelings of fulfilment at work shot up because, as we all know, people need to connect to people.

Here's a story that taught me the power of the written word when it doesn't go as planned. Early in my career as the national training manager for a luxury brand, I was responsible for buying the uniforms for 280 fragrance consultants. This turned out to be a costly experience.

The new uniform was shown at the company conference and everyone applauded, delighted with my choice. So far, so good (I thought, a little too soon). I followed this up with a letter to each fragrance consultant asking each person to tick a box confirming their uniform size (did you just get to the punch line?). I collated all 280 responses, added up the total for each dress size and placed the order, costing thousands.

You may not be surprised when I tell you that 34 per cent (yes, 34 per cent, this is not a typing error) of the new uniforms did not fit. Why? The simple answer is that people don't always mean what they say or say what they mean.

When I delved into why it had happened most of the 34 per cent who couldn't squeeze into their uniforms said similar things to me, such as:

- 'I really thought I would have dropped a dress size by the time it came' (just watching fitness DVDs doesn't work!)

- 'I didn't think you would have ordered from a company that made their sizes soooo small'.

I learnt a big lesson. I'll always remember that 34 per cent. I actually find it quite funny now, although it certainly wasn't at the time. Can you relate my story to something from your own experience? When has communication broken down for you because you dealt with what a person said or wrote (their actions) and missed what they were feeling (their attitude)? How would you do it differently next time? What did you learn?

You now have the knowledge and the tools to start to take control of your greatest asset – your mind. These tools will help you to influence and communicate effectively with others.

So let's pull this crucial chapter together: I was once asked to sum up the iceberg theory and the power of the Mind. My answer was:

> *Your 'I CAN' will empower you far more than your IQ.*

Whether you think you are capable of great things or whether you think you are not, you are right both times. What you think will always determine who you become.

Always tune into this immense power that is your attitude and be aware that with your thoughts you create your world and bring your life as it is now into existence. What lies behind you and what lies before you are small compared to what lies within you.

You cannot live a positive life with a negative mind so make your thoughts empowering ones that enhance you and set you up to live your best life yet. To change your attitude is to change your life.

chapter five

THE LAW
OF ATTRACTION IN
ACTION

I have spent the past thirty years learning about the universal law of attraction. This law states that not only are you the master of your thoughts but you *are* your thoughts. It's a neat idea but what does it mean? Essentially, your dominant thoughts are self-fulfilling so they create matching emotions. These emotions form your life as you know it – your thoughts create your world. If you find that idea a little scary consider the opportunities it presents! If you're unhappy with your life you can throw out the thoughts that are holding you back, replace them with new thoughts and get the life you want. And if you're happy with your life? Well you can make it even better.

THE MIND–BODY CONNECTION

I first became interested in the mind–body connection – the theory that the mind and body are inextricably connected – when I was just twenty years old and read *Psycho-Cybernetics* by Maxwell Maltz. Written in 1960, it was one of the first self-help books to define how our internal world (attitude and thoughts) creates our external world (actions and behaviours), and it paved the way for much of today's personal empowerment material.

The theory of that seminal book – in essence that your thoughts trigger your actions, your actions trigger your outcomes and your outcomes are your life – is at the very heart of my approach. Through my work as a success coach I have shared this principle with thousands of people and they have experienced extraordinary outcomes as a result. You will too when you introduce this universal law into your life.

So where do we start? With the following thought: whatever prominent and repetitive thoughts are going on in your mind, these will without doubt materialise in your life. No negotiation; it has always worked this way. The law of attraction is a universal law, or truth, that works every time and with everyone. It is exactly the same as the law of gravity. There are no exceptions. If I slipped and fell off the roof of a high building (unlikely I know) the law of gravity will ensure that I fall to the pavement below. And that, I expect, would be that. Happy or sad, rich or poor, believer or non-believer, young or old, healthy or poorly, kind or mean, it's irrelevant – if you slipped you would fall.

Gravity applies to all of us. You won't go to work one day, look out of your window and say to a colleague, 'Oh look, there's that nice man who works in marketing flying around the building. He must be on his lunch hour.' Gravity does not miss out Steve from marketing. And it's the same with the law of attraction; no one is exempt.

Thought boomerangs

The law of attraction dictates that your thoughts work in the same way as a boomerang. The thoughts you consistently think and 'throw out' into your world will come right back to you. They'll swing back and whack you on the head as emotions and create how you feel (hopefully the very true-to-life illustration opposite will help you remember that!).

It's a self-fulfilling prophecy. So what does that mean in practical terms?

- You cannot think thoughts of what you lack and what you think is wrong in your life and then attract a phenomenal and abundant life. If you think of lack and loss you will attract lack and loss.

- You cannot think worrying and anxious thoughts and then feel full of joy and happiness. Think of worry and anxiety and you will attract worry and anxiety.

Unfortunately, too many people use the law of attraction to focus on *negative* events. Here are some examples:

- I don't want to be hurt again.

- I don't want someone to take advantage of my ideas.

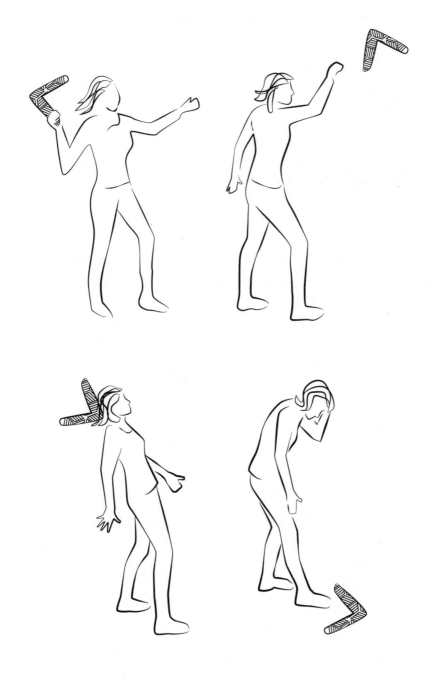

- I don't want to miss out on promotion again.

- I don't want to get this wrong and mess up again.

This type of thinking can so easily become a habit with the inevitable result that the person gets back, time and time again, exactly what they don't want. The mind is neutral and will only accept what it is told. So if you keep thinking about what you don't want, you'll just attract and get more of it. If you expect to be disappointed, you won't disappoint yourself (think about it!).

To make matters worse, thinking 'I don't want' stifles the positive energy of ideas, solutions and imagination, blocking the energy you need to create the life you desire. The law of attraction works by attracting to you what you think. So everything that you think about and speak about your mind assumes are things 'you want'. So it follows that:

> *You cannot think thoughts of having a phenomenal and abundant life and attract back a life of boredom and apathy.*

This is the positive side of thought boomerangs. Make the effort to shift all your focus, thoughts and the images you see in your mind to what you *do* want and your thought boomerangs will attract it to you. Pack your days with thoughts of abundance, hope, belief, passion, excitement, gratitude, appreciation and fun, and you'll attract back all those positive emotions, ideas, opportunities and solutions. The list of positive emotions is endless. You get to decide and you get to choose. It's your life that we're working on here.

Decide now to focus only on what's right in your life, because:

- if you think of what's fabulous in your life you'll attract more of what's fabulous right back to you

- if you think of what's good and right in your life you will attract more of what's good and right in your life back to you.

This is why I started this book by asking you to focus on what's right in your life *now*. Start on a solid foundation of positivity and you will attract more of the good stuff back to you. On page 105 I'll ask you to put pen to paper and think about this in concrete terms but first let's look at the energy that is created by those thought boomerangs.

Thought creates energy – positive and negative

Be under no illusion, whatever you focus on constantly you will move towards. Right now you are precisely what you have consistently thought about up until this moment in time. Your thought boomerangs have an energy force that is either positive or negative, depending on your focus, therefore thought boomerangs are either:

- **Positive, life-empowering, self-fulfilling prophecies**
  These will give you positive energy and pleasurable
  emotions such as happiness, joy, laughter, passion,
  confidence, self-worth, gratitude, hope, inspiration,
  imagination, prosperity, etc. And as a consequence
  you'll experience high levels of self-confidence,
  self-belief and self-worth.

Or

- **Negative, life-diluting, self-fulfilling prophecies**
  These will give you negative energy and painful
  emotions such as frustration, depression, self-doubt,
  anger, grumpiness, worry, apathy, etc. And as a
  consequence you will experience low or non-existent
  levels of self-confidence, self-belief and self-worth.

So which will you choose? Ask yourself if where you are
now emotionally is where you want to be, because self-
fulfilling prophecies are bringing your future hurtling
towards you at speed. You need to make sure you like
what's coming your way!

The good news is that it is all in your hands (in your
thoughts actually).

HOW ARE YOU NOW?

How would you describe the moods and emotions you
fill your days with? Overall, how would you describe your
present attitude? Consider this in the knowledge that

your thought boomerangs come right back to you with either good thoughts and good emotions or bad thoughts and bad emotions. The following exercise will help you pinpoint – and if necessary change – the emotions that are familiar to you. It can have a tremendous impact on your motivation levels and desire to make positive changes.

EXERCISE

Your Attitude and Emotions MOT

Below are most of the emotions available to you.

In your notebook, write down the words which best describe your current emotional state (this is for your benefit alone so be truthful with yourself):

Positive emotions

Optimistic	Joyous	Fun	Happy
Excited	Empowered	Passionate	Inspired
Enthusiastic	Content	Calm	Serene
Trusting	Carefree	Satisfied	Fulfilled
Courageous	Harmony	Peaceful	Kindness
Empathetic	Determined	Thankful	Strong
Grateful	Trusting	Confident	Secure
Compassion	Self-sufficient	Self-pride	Content
Decisive	Satisfied		

Negative emotions

Pessimistic	Sad	Jealous	Angry
Blaming	Regretful	Miserable	Resentful
Worried	Apathetic	Anxious	Weary
Fearful	Lonely	Inadequate	Insecure
Rejected	Overwhelmed	Foolish	Cynical
Hostile	Insignificant	Confused	Suspicious
Envy	Embarrassed	Vanity	Dissatisfied
Complacency	Irritable	Annoyed	Boastful
Bitter	Indecision	Despondent	Dejected
Discontent	Judgemental		

You have now exposed the emotions and feelings you are filling your days with. Do you like them? Do you want to keep them? It's obvious to see which emotions are your friends and which the enemy. All thoughts boomerang back to you as self-fulfilling prophecies from what you are focusing on and thinking about.

When I ask people I coach to do the exercise above here's what happens:

- Those who select mostly from the positive list of emotions are inspired and motivated to keep doing what they are doing and further improve their focus and positive thoughts.

- Those who select mostly from the negative list feel despondent and say 'I can't believe that's me – it's like looking in the mirror and not liking who I've become'. If you feel the same then STOP! This is not 'who you are', it is what you have become as a result of your thoughts and focus up to this point in time. Your future starts now. In this minute you can decide to change your focus and thinking and start to attract back to you any of the positive emotions shown here. Wouldn't NOW be a good time to start?

Your continual focus and thoughts easily become habits and the foundations of the life you are living now, but I want you to realise that the moods and emotions that fill your days now do not have to be the same ones that will fill your days in the future. You are in charge of your thoughts and this means that you are in charge of your emotions, actions and outcomes. You can choose to have any emotions you want to experience in your life. You only need to focus your thoughts on the positive and they'll bounce right into your life.

> *Negativity cannot survive without your participation and permission.*

This is not something to take lightly; this is a vital strategy that will make a big difference to you and a massive difference to your life.

You should know this well by now, but just to recap, when you want to feel:

- happy, think happy thoughts

- miserable, think miserable thoughts

- confident, think confident thoughts

- excited, think exciting thoughts

- bored, think boring thoughts

- energised, think energising thoughts

- tired, think tiring thoughts

- fit, think fitness thoughts

- successful, think successful thoughts

- fulfilled, think fulfilling thoughts

- fabulous, think of your fabulousness!

So many feelings and so little time! The list of emotions you can choose between is endless and every single feeling is there for you to select from. It's like flicking through a brochure or catalogue to choose whatever you want. You wouldn't order clothes that don't suit you would you? So why on earth would you choose thoughts and emotions that don't make you feel good or look good? (Negative emotions show on our faces just as much as positive ones.)

People often ask me, 'What do you think is stopping me from getting what I want?' My answer is always the same – your thoughts! Remind yourself daily that just as you choose what you want to buy from an online retailer you can choose your emotions in exactly the same way. It's a moods and emotions click and collect.

In Chapter 10, I will share my recipe for creating a positive mood.

You control you

You're in control here so it's up to you to become very aware of times when you allow your thoughts to be negative. An example might be when you focus on what you think is wrong in your life or on what you feel is lacking. Choose to do this and you will have diluted your happiness and personal feelings of success and fulfilment.

At this point you may be thinking, 'That's all very well but you don't know how hard things are for me.' You're right: I don't. But the core message I want to get across to you stays the same irrespective of your circumstances: you become what you focus on. Focusing on what is wrong will just attract more of that to you. You cannot move out of a negative state unless you move out of the feelings that got you there in the first place. If that feels like a wakeup call for you that's great. As you've already discovered, motivation brought on by desperation creates empowering actions.

I say this from experience. A few years ago I found myself in very difficult personal circumstances, and feeling negative was an easy option and one that people around me sympathised with. (Many find sympathy comforting; lots of 'poor you' but be aware, this will keep you in the past and will not propel you into the future where you need to be heading.) But I did not stay in this negative state for long. Did it take immense effort? Yes of course it did (masses at times). But I did change my state from negative to positive by changing my focus and you can too. When you are able to do this you will feel in control of your life, empowered and positive emotions will reward you tenfold for the effort.

> *Tough times do not last:*
> *tough people do.*

I believe in the saying: fall five times, get back up six times. When I experience a 'fall', I put my energy into falling forwards. If you do this it throws you into what is before you; into solutions and new opportunities and not backwards into the problem. You're in control here so decide to release your full potential by making your predominant thoughts and focus positive and your attitude an empowering one. Believe that your life is meant to be abundant in all areas.

Positive or negative boomerangs – your choice

So which are you going to choose? Will you focus on positive or negative thoughts throughout your day? I know this is a no-brainer but I want you to decide and commit to the right answer.

One situation and two perspectives

Let's look at an example that most of us can relate to: the break-up of a relationship. I want you to imagine two differing perspectives, one positive and one negative, so you can compare the impact each person's attitude had on the outcome.

Someone with a positive attitude will search for the things they can learn from the experience so that it will not be repeated. Their thoughts, therefore, will be along the following lines:

- 'It's good to be out of that relationship because it didn't make me happy or enhance my life.'

- 'What can I take from this experience that will help me create the life I want?'

- 'What can I now learn from this so I will start to feel happier more quickly and put this experience firmly in my past?'

I used to have a fridge magnet which said: In life it is better to travel alone than be badly accompanied. This will ring true for those with a positive attitude. They will learn what it is they want to be different in their next relationship (because they *will* have one) and will focus on thoughts like these:

- 'Good, I'm now free to meet someone who will love and respect me. Until then I can do a great job loving and respecting myself.'

- 'What do I hope my next relationship will be like? What am I looking for?'

- 'I believe I will attract a person into my life who is caring, funny and loving.'

Someone with a positive attitude will learn from any challenging life experience so that they do not repeat it again. Then they take what they have learnt from the experience and move forward in their life. Their focus is positive so life-affirming emotions will boomerang back to them (feelings of being in control, optimism and self-worth) and for their next relationship I imagine they'll choose well.

Now imagine the same scenario through the eyes of someone with a negative attitude. They will be inclined to think like this:

- 'It's my fault, it must be me; I don't deserve anything more.'

- 'This is my lot because it's all I ever get – bad luck in relationships.'

- 'I won't ever be in another relationship again and I'll stay on my own forever.'

Their thinking and focus is negative; so what emotions will boomerang back to them? Life-diluting emotions and feelings of sadness, bitterness, rejection, misery, envy and low self-worth. And their next relationship? It's unlikely to be great. And that in itself should give this person the motivation to reframe the experience as a positive lesson so that they can move on with their life just as an optimist would.

You know that whatever you think about and make your dominant repetitive thoughts will come back to you in your life as emotions and feelings, actions and experience. So take full responsibility and ownership for your personal focus and thought boomerangs. It can change your life immeasurably for the better.

YOUR MIND DOES NOT JUDGE

Your mind does not have an opinion. It will not judge you, put your thoughts through some sort of positive filter system or decide for you that your thoughts are negative and unworthy of you. Nor will it tell you that they must immediately be changed or deleted. Nope, it cannot do this for you. You have 100 per cent control and ownership here – thank goodness.

Remember, how you choose to live your life is determined not so much by what life brings to you as by the attitude you bring to life. And not so much by what happens to you or has happened to you but by the way you interpret what has happened. When you think thoughts like 'I'll never do that', 'I've failed again', 'Why do I always meet the wrong person?' 'Why do people always let me down?' 'They'll never give me the promotion', 'All I ever get is bad luck', the universal law of attraction does not judge. It is neither 'on your side' nor against you. If you think it you'll attract it. Boomerangs, remember.

Is what you tell yourself real or imagined?

Just as the mind does not judge, it does not differentiate between what is real and what is imagined. It will simply try to move you in the direction of the things you focus on. Therefore if there is something you wish to have, be or do, just hold that thought, repeat it many times and hold it constantly in your focus. Imagine and see what you want with total belief and by the law of attraction you will get back to you the positive energy, ideas, belief, hope, passion, people and opportunities you need to make what you imagined a reality for you. By the power of thought boomerangs everything you require *will* be attracted back to you.

And if you're one of those people – there are many I know – who think about things that have not happened yet and focus on imagined worries, problems and concerns, remind yourself that if you keep doing this they *will* happen. So stop now before it becomes a negative, self-fulfilling prophecy. Replace those imagined negative thoughts with positive ones that will make you feel fabulous.

The positive power of your imagination and the ability to see and attract into your life what you desire but don't have yet is such an immensely powerful strategy that Chapter 8 is devoted to this subject.

DON'T DWELL ON NEGATIVE EVENTS FROM THE PAST

You now know that your mind will not play judge and filter your thoughts, it will only accept them. So if you decide to press 'replay' once again to think about things from the past that went wrong for you, you know you'll attract more of the same back to you. Don't do it. Would you jump in your car and try to drive in reverse gear for the entire journey home? No I thought not.

So let me ask you, why go through life in reverse, constantly thinking back to things you didn't like, didn't get or that didn't work out? You will only attract back to you more of what has gone before. Don't look backwards and live life in reverse gear unless that's where you want to go back to.

You know deep down that when you say to yourself repeatedly things like 'I'll never meet someone special', 'I never get recognised for doing a good job', 'They don't appreciate me or value what I do', 'I'll never learn how to do this' or 'I'll never have enough money to buy that and go there', your focus is on what you cannot achieve and this negative belief will drain your confidence, passion, energy and creative ideas. You will kill off great, empowering emotions. You and only you have stopped great things coming to you. It's not a coincidence, it's the law of attraction working – you know you become what you think about constantly so decide to focus on the positive.

Don't just throw in the odd positive day

In my work I've come across more people than I should who live their lives on auto-pilot, reacting to what life throws at them and they just throw in the odd good day here and there, and a sprinkling of positive thoughts to keep them going. What a waste of potentially great days.

If you think you can live your life like this, with the odd positive day thrown in, think of the analogy of trying to use your mobile phone when the battery is dead. However desperate you are to make a call it will not happen if there is no energy charge. You operate in exactly the same way. To work to your full potential requires a full positive energy surge every single day. If you allow your energy to get too low or empty it will take wasted time to charge back up. It's far more sensible to keep a full battery of positive energy, continually adding daily top-ups. It's quicker, easier and life is immeasurably happier that way.

THE CAN'T DO CLUB

There are many people who live their lives with a 'Can't Do' attitude. I expect you know some (and if you are one, take heart – it's never too late to change). You will often hear them say things like this:

- 'See, I told you I couldn't do it and that it wouldn't work.'

- 'I can't do this because…'

- 'It's not my fault I can't do this.'

It's the law of attraction working again in the universe. If you see life as a series of problems, that's precisely what you attract, more problems.

Everything begins with a thought

Let's take the example of someone thinking and focusing on 'I'll never get the job I want'. As a direct consequence of continually focusing on the negative (thinking there's not enough jobs, too many people are going for the same job, others are better qualified and more experienced, etc.), their thoughts become their emotional state and their subsequent actions. This impacts how they behave when they are given an opportunity to impress, for example in an interview. Their doubts and negative thoughts kill the opportunity. The result is a diluting, self-fulfilling prophecy. And they'll tell you, 'See I told you this always happens to me, I never get the job I want and again the job has gone to someone more qualified, experienced, better…'

They chose to focus on 'never getting the job they want' and they proved themselves right.

Another example of this kind of thinking is: 'I'll never meet anyone special'. Someone who has a negative opinion of their personal qualities and their ability to attract a suitable partner is bound to attract the wrong sort of person – or they will not attract anyone at all. They thought they would never meet anyone special and by God they are right! Their focus is singularly on how it could not happen and not on how it could happen.

If you relate to either of these examples then you know that you and you alone created the outcome. But if you choose to focus on 'I can' and 'It will happen' then this positive thought, based on faith rather than fear, will also self-fulfil. It's up to you.

Always remember the mind is neutral to our thoughts. It does not judge or filter your thoughts, it only accepts them.

EXERCISE

Turn I can't into I can

People who feel life is a struggle and that success eludes them are often those who focus on what they can't do, should have done and could have done. This exercise will help you learn to avoid this kind of thinking.

Think back to three personal examples where you focused on 'I can't do', 'I can't have', 'I can't be'. Write them down in your notebook.

1. I can't do...

2. I can't have...

3. I can't be...

Now change each of these old limiting beliefs and rethink and reword them. For example, successful people constantly think in terms of: I will, I am and I can. And focus on what they can do and on life's positive possibilities. For example, 'I can't lose weight' could be turned into 'I can lose weight and I'm excited about eating healthily'. Now it's your turn:

1. I can...

2. I will...

3. I am...

> 6 Whether you think you can or whether you
> think you can't. You are right 9
> **HENRY FORD**

YOU REAP WHAT YOU SOW

We all know this saying. Like attracts like. Here's a true story that illustrates the point well.

A few years ago a company booked me to coach Penny, one of their senior executives. They felt her attitude was negative and limiting her progression. (I'm often told 'it's an attitude problem' when I'm asked to coach someone.) As Penny walked into the room, I could tell she did so with a heavy heart. This is exciting for me as I know what a massive difference a Mind Makeover can make to someone with a negative outlook.

Within a short time we were chatting comfortably so we began to explore the reasons why Penny was behaving in a particular way in her role, what she was actually doing and how she was feeling. This is the 'why', 'what' and 'how' approach I outlined in Chapter 1. Penny told me that she'd had a problem with her line manager, at which point she became very passionate and demonstrative, recounting in minute detail what her manager had done, said, the impact it had had on her, whom she blamed, how unfair it was ... She eventually stopped, took a deep breath and sighed (it was an Oscar-worthy performance).

At this point I wondered why the company training director hadn't told me about this issue prior to the coaching session. Yet, from experience, I guessed what was coming next. I asked Penny when this had happened. And the answer? Two years before! Penny had chosen to carry this negative, life-diluting baggage around with her for two years, replaying the experience hundreds of times in her mind. She had focused all her energy on pressing the replay button hundreds of times and telling anyone who would listen what had happened to her: she had been passed over for promotion and the job she deserved and it was so unfair. Think about what the law of attraction had boomeranged back to her and how it had made her life for the past two years. Frustrated and stressed I imagine.

Obviously she had not been experiencing happiness, success and fulfilment in her work but neither had she seen or seized any other opportunities to feel good because she was totally focused on the negative emotions of blame and self-pity. I coached her to change what she was thinking about, getting her to focus on controlling her attitude and the positive thoughts that would get her to where she wanted to be and to how she wanted to feel.

At the end of our coaching sessions she wrote what she called her six rules of life. They're great and Penny was only too happy for me to share them:

Six rules of life

1. I love being responsible for my thoughts and they are positive and empowering.

2. I'm fully in control of my mind. It's mine alone.

3. I seize all opportunities and if the opportunities I want aren't out there I'll create them.

4. I excel at what I'm passionate about.

5. I live my full potential every day. I'm happy, successful and fulfilled.

6. I appreciate and celebrate what's good in my life now!

Another successful Mind Makeover!

So, how did I get Penny to come to these powerful conclusions and to such a positive point in her life?

WIIFM – WHAT'S IN IT FOR ME?

The answer is in asking yourself, 'what's in it for me?' or WIIFM for short. There is nothing more powerful and motivating for most people than an injection of WIIFM. As I have shared, it's about the self-gain and self-benefits of taking positive action and creating change. WIIFM will make you highly motivated to make positive shifts in your attitude and keen to take massive action.

In the next exercise I'll ask you to write down your own WIIFMs but here are some examples to inspire you and get you thinking:

Getting out of a career rut Feelings of courage, excitement; meeting new people and having new experiences; more money

Losing excess weight Feeling in control, better fitting clothes, greater confidence, pride, achievement, success

Reducing negativity Feeling more joy, happiness, hope, confidence and self-worth

Clearing your clutter (house/office) Being able to find things easily, save time, feel organised and in control, able to prioritise, gain a sense of achievement

Tackling your anger Live in the present and the future not the past, learn from it, knowing you can change your focus and so change your emotional state from negative to positive

When the gain is big enough (WIIFM) then the pain of taking action disappears. And not changing becomes 'not an option'.

EXERCISE

List your WIIFMs

Ask yourself 'What is the gain for me? How will I benefit from putting in the effort to change and improve my attitude, thoughts, focus, emotions and actions? What impact would this have on me, on how I feel and what I achieve?'

Write down five personal WIIFMs. Think about emotions or actions you've been putting off changing.

Tune into your feelings

Of course, in order to improve your thoughts and focus you need to tune in to them. I looked at this earlier in the chapter but let's get practical here.

Over the years I've met many people whose attitude to their day is set by how they view a small element of it. For example, their day starts badly (their opinion, their attitude): they slept through the alarm, it was raining, they got soaked on the way in to work ... And they allow those first ninety minutes to frame their entire day so that it spirals out of control and into a negative pit called a rotten day. A lady I used to work with would greet me in the morning three days out of five with the words, 'Oh God, I can't wait for it to be 5.30 p.m.!' Why throw your precious life away in this way.

Tune into your feelings: they are your constant guide and tell you if you are being your own best friend or enemy. How you feel is a direct result of what you are thinking and focusing on, good or bad, so don't throw a day of your life away because of a bad thirty-minute journey to work. Stop the chain reaction. You can because it starts with one thought – yours. It's the law of attraction in action and a self-fulfilling prophecy. Start your day over again and change what you are focusing on. How you feel will move from negative to positive in a second (in one thought).

EXERCISE

Dealing with negative thoughts

Some people tell me they struggle with letting go of negative opinions and experiences in their past. Do you relate to this personally? This exercise will help.

- Tune into any negative thoughts you constantly focus on. List three things you hold on to as sustained negative thoughts.

- What are you attracting back to you with your negative thoughts?

- What changes will you make?

- Now, tune into positive, empowering thoughts you constantly focus on. List five things you hold on to as measured and sustained positive thoughts.

- What are you attracting back to you when you do this?

It goes without saying really, but consider what you're attracting back to yourself with those negative thoughts – and stop! Concentrate on the positive empowering thoughts that will make every day count.

There is no such thing as an unimportant day.

IS YOUR LIFE FULL OF COMPLIMENTS OR COMPLAINTS?

Remember we looked at this in detail in Chapter 4. I once complimented a sales assistant after exemplary service. Keen to pass on this positive feedback, I asked if her department manager was on the shop floor (this is a retail expression, which if you are not in retail sounds as though the manager has had too much vino).

Off she went to find her manager and from a distance I could see an annoyed-looking lady walking towards me. The manager stopped abruptly in front of me (still stony faced) and with an enormous sigh said, 'I'm the department manager. What's the problem?'

I saw words in bold flashing lights over her head saying: URGENT NEED OF MIND MAKEOVER. I immediately changed from being a satisfied customer to my day job as a success coach. I answered with a smile, 'Well Mrs J YOU are the problem. You assumed I had a complaint and came to me with a negative attitude. I wanted to compliment you on your staff.' (She actually wore a name badge. With her attitude I don't think I'd be volunteering my name to folks. I'd go undercover.) She was shocked out of her negative attitude and immediately became more approachable.

Let me ask you again: do you focus on compliments or complaints throughout your day? As always, the choice is yours.

Are you spending your time being grateful for and appreciating what you have in your life or are you spending your time complaining about what you don't like, don't want and don't have in your life?

- If you are complaining about things in your life then you will just attract back to you more things to complain about.

- If you are praising things and being grateful for all you have in your life then you will attract back to you more things to be grateful for.

EXERCISE

What do you appreciate in your life?

Stop and focus on what you feel immensely appreciative of and grateful for in your life now. And if you have trouble with that, think back to those young women at Centrepoint – there are always things to be grateful for.

- **Write a 'gratitude list':** I am so happy and grateful for the following (go for ten).

I'm aware many people struggle with this – to begin with – so here are some examples:

My health, mind and body...
My good friends, my wonderful children...
The opportunities I can create and seize...
My hobbies, my talent, my fabulousness...
Seeing a rainbow, a sunrise, a beautiful view
My crazy dog!
Whatever grabs you...

When you write out your gratitude list your feel-good factor will shoot up and it will lift your spirits quicker than anything I know – and you potentially have hundreds of things to write down here. Keep thinking and keep adding. Many people I work with choose to buy a beautiful journal or notebook to record all their gratitude lists in. It creates a powerful source of feel-good, inspiration and motivation, and you can keep it to hand at all times. If you don't do this already – try it. It works.

SIXTY THOUSAND THOUGHTS A DAY

Researchers tell us that we each have around sixty thousand thoughts every day. The majority of those thoughts will be exactly the same as the ones we had the day before and the day before that and the day before that. But what if you were to consciously think just a hundred positive thoughts each day? In fact, just ten would have a phenomenal impact for many people. That's not too much to ask is it? Look again at the list of positive emotions on page 105 and select the ones you want to focus on and think about to attract those emotions back to you.

How to police your thoughts

Now that you understand the immense power of your thoughts you're probably wondering how on earth you can possibly monitor all your thoughts to ensure that negativity isn't creeping into your day.

It's simple. You check in with yourself often and ask yourself: 'How do I feel right now? How would I describe my mood and emotions?' Your answer will immediately tell you whether your thoughts are positive (worth keeping and repeating) or negative (bin and get rid of).

I must stress that you don't have to tune in to every single thought because often you will be on 'automatic pilot' and your thoughts will be positive and habitual. What you are committing to here is a new acute sense of awareness so that when you start to think thoughts that dilute your well-being a big warning bell goes off in your head with neon flashing lights saying 'negativity alert';

stop now and replace immediately with a life-empowering thought.

Decide now to monitor and tune into your emotions and feelings throughout your day. Ask yourself 'How do I feel?' 'What one emotion describes my mood *now?*' Your answers tell you what emotions you are feeling and these come from what you are thinking. There's your answer.

Your answers will tell you if you are setting yourself up for a great day or not. Never forget, you can start your day over any time you choose to by immediately changing your thoughts and focus away from things that make you miserable. When you ask yourself 'How am I feeling now?' and your answer involves words such as 'worried, sad, disappointed, let down, frustrated, anxious', stop doing what you are doing. Think very carefully about what you are focusing on and thinking about to create these horrible feelings, feelings you do not want in your life. Focus on and think about why you are thinking these thoughts. Understand the 'why' behind the 'what'.

Understand your thoughts and learn from them. What are you basing your thoughts on and why? Is it your perception or your reality? Now replace negative thoughts with conscious positive thoughts that enhance your life, versus diluting it. Think thoughts that make you feel happy, fulfilled, proud, joyous, grateful, loved and other positively empowering emotions.

Remember, happiness is a daily decision, and so is being miserable.

EXERCISE

Empowering emotions

Try this right now and feel and experience the empowering emotions you'll get back. Think about the following emotions:

- **happy** – write down one thing that you feel very happy about

- **proud** – write down one thing that you feel very proud about

- **grateful** – write down one thing that you feel very grateful for

- **contented** – write down one thing that you feel content about

- **excited** – write down one thing that you feel very excited about

- **passionate** – write down one thing that you feel very passionate about.

When you choose your thoughts you choose your emotions, feelings and the subsequent actions you will take every single day you do this: you're creating your fabulous world one day at a time. Why not say to yourself 'just for today' I will feel...' and then run through this exercise in your mind and 'feel' your answers? Give them meaning beyond the words. See them; visualise yourself being in the emotion and think them into existence.

Consciously choose your thoughts to enable you to achieve what you want in your life because what you think about you bring about in your world. Your dominant thoughts are the mirror of the life you are creating for yourself.

Tell yourself often:

- I and I alone control my thoughts and with my thoughts I create my world. I deserve to love my world, starting right now!

- I will think my life into existence and it will be absolutely the life I want to live now.

- I alone am the master of my thoughts. My mind is mine and mine alone. No one can enter in without my permission.

In the next chapter, I'm going to show you how to program your thoughts to achieve further control of your mind and give you even more joy and success.

chapter six

COMPUTER SOFTWARE FOR YOUR MIND

What holds you back from getting the life you want; from using the power of your thoughts to take charge of your life? For many the answer is the stress of living in the 21st century. There's just *so much* to think about! Yes there is, but, as I hope you now realise, the answer lies in how you use your thoughts to shape your world.

The strategy outlined in this chapter – I call it my 'mind computer' strategy – is designed to help you focus on what is important; what will move you towards a more successful life. Many of my Mind Makeover clients have told me this strategy really helped them to reduce their stress levels and introduce feelings of calmness and control.

USE YOUR SOFTWARE

Comparing the mind to a computer is a useful analogy when thinking about how the mind operates. For a computer to work it must have power, via an electricity socket or battery. The 'electricity' or energy of your mind comes from one power source only, your thoughts. And dependent upon whether your thoughts are positive or negative, they will give you:

- a positive energy surge – positive thoughts generating positive energy; or

- a power cut – negative energy from negative thoughts, which prevents good things happening to you.

Each of us has an endless stream of thoughts day in day out. Remember those sixty thousand thoughts per day I mentioned in the previous chapter: imagine sixty thousand emails in our inbox when we switched on our office or home computer in the morning – we'd soon burn out.

However, in addition to what is going on in our own minds, technological innovation means we are constantly being bombarded with data from various sources and are communicating in numerous different ways. In less than a minute your mobile phone can ring then your landline, just as an email pings through and all the while your partner or child is standing beside you trying to have a conversation. For many of us, information overload has become the norm; for some, communication is literally 24/7. I've worked with many executives who have global responsibilities and they are expected to be available as necessary, irrespective of the time in the UK.

Given the sorts of pressures we're under these days, it's easy to become overloaded, therefore it's essential to take charge of all that information before you begin drowning in it. In Chapter 3 we looked at how to prioritise tasks when things feel overwhelming, but how do you deal with the vast volume of thoughts, conscious or unconscious, that hurtle your way day in day out?

YOUR MIND COMPUTER

Let's go back to the simple analogy of a computer. What positive impact would it have on you if you used your mind like the filing system on a computer, organising and filing all the thoughts and data that come your way? What if you also applied this approach to all the information that you have stored inside your mind for years, including your beliefs and your life experiences so far? It's an intriguing thought – and, believe it or not, a practical one. It's a simple approach that works in exactly the same way as organising the files on your hard drive and email inbox.

Let me ask you a question:

- How are you able to quickly and easily find the information you want on your computer?

The simple answer is that you classify your information, separating it into different files, and then name each file individually so you're able to search for what you want and find it quickly. You command your computer to search for the file name and within a split second the information you requested pops up.

Imagine how much more in control you would feel if you were to do the same with your mind – you could throw all the stuff you don't need in the waste bin and access all the positive thoughts you need in a split second.

Your software commands

In order to use your mind in this way you need to sort your conscious thoughts into four broad categories, which tie in with commands that you would commonly use on your computer.

The four commands are:

- File & Save

- Delete & Dump

- Mute

- Review & Edit

The purpose of each command is as follows:

- **File & Save:** to store all your positive and empowering thoughts and experiences.

- **Delete & Dump:** to remove permanently all the rubbish (thoughts and experiences) and negativity you do not want to keep.

- **Mute:** to turn down the sound when you do not want to absorb negative chat. For example, when you are in the company of someone negative.

- **Review & Edit:** to enable you to replay, at any time, personal experiences that you can learn from in order to improve similar experiences in the future.

Filing information and thoughts in this way creates order and control in your mind. When you want specific information and, most importantly, specific thoughts to help you to create positive emotions (confidence, self-belief, passion, hope and so on) this is how you find and access what you want quickly and easily. It really is this simple.

Use the mind computer strategy throughout your day and you will de-clutter your mind immeasurably. You will feel empowered and 'in charge' of your thoughts and emotions. Same person, same life, yet now you will be feeling calm, confident and in control.

Let's go through each command in detail.

Command: File & Save

This is where you put all those important experiences and achievements – those things that have made you feel fulfilled, proud, happy and successful. See it as your own 'personal empowerment file'.

EXERCISE

Your personal empowerment file

This is your chance to really pin down the key positive experiences and achievements that have shaped you. For example, winning a top prize at school, running a 10K race, getting on the course you dreamed of, getting a promotion, getting to grips with a new hobby (I said a hobby not hubby) ... the potential answers are endless and, of course, personal to you.

- Write down ten experiences in your life so far that you would store in this file.

- What emotions do these experiences trigger (is it confidence, belief, success, personal pride and fulfilment)? Think back to how this made you feel at the time; picture and replay it happening again. Try to see it, feel it and bring the experience back to life in your mind.

- How does this make you feel now? If you do not experience as powerful and positive a feeling from the memory as you did when it actually happened just repeat what you are doing a few times and the feelings and emotions you experienced will bounce back to you.

Once you have 'filed & saved' the thoughts you wish to keep then you can search in seconds for the information you want. Information linked to a memory will trigger the positive emotions you want to feel again. Simply ask yourself, 'What have I done, what was it I achieved, what positive experiences have I stored in my "personal empowerment file" that will help me re-live this positive emotion?'

The information you pull from your 'file' will give you all the positive emotions you want to live your day-to-day life by, such as self-belief, confidence, passion, feel-good, pride, imagination, inspiration, motivation, etc. You can pick from a wide range of positive emotional experiences – from feeling deeply loved to enormous pride at a job well done – they are all there waiting for you to experience once again. The list is endless and it's your list. You can access it any time you choose. How great is that!

It's like having your very own search engine to find whatever you need to feel fabulous and confident in seconds. But be sure you ask for what you want and not what you don't want. Think about it this way: if you want to use the internet to book a holiday in Spain you wouldn't type 'plumbers' in the search box would you? Obviously not. Instead of sipping a chilled white wine at a beach bar in Spain, you'd be at home with a plumber repairing your pipes! So why in life when you want to experience positive feelings of happiness, fulfilment and success would you focus on anything that does the opposite?

Remember, in life what's wrong is always available and so is what's right. With this file you are able to access things that are right now in your life and also memories of what's been right in your past. You can focus and think about them and as a consequence generate and repeat the positive emotions you felt back then. The same emotions you want to recreate for your day, now, today.

Keep a journal

In my career I have met many inspirational and highly successful individuals who each use this strategy of storing positive experiences in their mind. Many of them back this up with a physical copy too.

For ten years I was a judge of the Cosmetic and Fragrance Industry's Supreme Beauty Consultant Award. It's a prestigious and coveted award, and involves a series of 'mystery shops' and interviews, with the six regional winners out of a potential eight thousand entrants going on to a panel interview in London. Each year, without exception, every one of the six talented individuals I met and interviewed at this stage of the selection process arrived with some form of 'personal empowerment file' tucked under their arm. These comprised everything from specifics of their personal achievements, congratulatory letters they had received, details of highly successful events they had organised and so on.

As a success coach this was no surprise to me. Each and every winner used this strategy to give them maximum advantage and a continual and empowering focus so they were plugged into positive energy, fully charged up and bursting with confidence, pride and self-belief.

And I want you to do exactly the same for yourself. Try it. Do it. Keep doing it and form this positive habit.

Command: Delete & Dump

Let me ask you a question: why would you store happiness-diluting thoughts, memories and experiences in your mind? Why would any of us want to keep any thoughts in our minds that do not make us feel great? These are the sort of memories that, when replayed, bring up negative emotions and make us feel thoroughly miserable.

Imagine you went to the cinema to watch a film and at the end you said to your friend 'That was a horrible film, it's made me feel thoroughly miserable', would you then suggest going back the next night to watch it over again? No of course you wouldn't. So why would you repeat an experience that makes you feel miserable? Why focus on things that make you feel sad? It's the same as going night after night to the cinema to watch a depressing film.

So what's the answer? Let's start with the here and now (before we look at deleting and dumping all that useless stuff that you already have filed away). When something doesn't go to plan or something happens that makes you feel miserable, ask yourself this: 'Will this bother me in a month's time?' The answer is usually something along the lines of, 'No ... I probably won't even remember it.'

So why wait four weeks to get that feeling? Why wait when you can feel the way you say you'll feel in four weeks' time, right now? Delete and dump the negative focus. Change your thoughts and you change your moods, change your moods and you change your world. You know all about the law of attraction. Use it. Once you've deleted that negative state, throw out as many positive thought boomerangs as you can. You'll get an abundance of positive thoughts, emotions and feelings bouncing straight back to you.

As well as dealing this way with negative situations and thoughts as they crop up you need to throw out all the negative thoughts, information, data and experiences from your past that dilute your joy. I mean delete *all* of it; even the debilitating memories and thoughts you've kept for years, just in case you want to bring them back in to your life at some point. You don't and you won't so bin them *now*. I practise this constantly, and to make it even more powerful I imagine them dropping into a delete bin, just like the one on my computer screen. Let me repeat myself: delete and dump *anything* that doesn't make you feel good, great or phenomenal in your world and is not giving you the life you want. Do not replay past negative experiences, for example when you say, 'Why does this always happen to me?' (it doesn't), 'Why do I always get passed over for promotion?' (you don't). The commands called 'delete' and 'dump' are waiting for you to use. Remember, thoughts materialise into reality – your reality.

Just as you, and only you, can decide what to store in your personal empowerment file, you alone will know what to delete and dump from your mind and your life.

EXERCISE

Delete & dump

- Write down three current negative thinking habits that you will now delete and dump from your mind and focus.

- Done it? Good. How do you feel now? Ask yourself, 'What's in it for me?'

- Now write down five past experiences you will now delete and dump from your mind and focus.

- How do you feel now you have done this? Ask yourself again, 'What's in it for me?'

Don't share it!

Even worse than storing negative thoughts and experiences and replaying them over and over again, is sharing them with anyone willing to listen. Put together two people sharing their negative experiences – and, believe me, a lot of people do this – and they'll make each other feel even worse than they did to begin with (particularly if they're also sharing a couple of glasses of Chardonnay at the same time!). I call this negative synergy. Synergy is commonly used to describe something positive – how the interaction of two or more forces have a combined effect that is greater than the sum of the parts. *Negative* synergy is a concept that I think illustrates perfectly what I see often in both business and social situations: two negative energy forces meeting and becoming *weaker* because their combined misery dissipates joy and happiness for both. Why anyone would choose to do this is beyond me.

Getting people to understand the immense power of synergy is an important part of my work, as it's one of the most effective strategies for utilising 'people power' (a company's greatest asset) and growing teams and companies. I often tell groups, in business or in life:

- positive synergy is common sense but is not always common practice; whereas

- negative synergy is common practice yet is definitely not common sense.

Here's a real example of negative synergy. Imagine a group of beauty consultants who work for one cosmetic brand in a department store. Each has their own unique personality, attitude and belief system. Julie doesn't think Robert pulls his weight; Robert thinks Julie is too full of herself; Susan thinks she's the best salesperson who's ever been in the team; and Julie thinks Susan doesn't even realise that she *is* in a team and works under the illusion that the only thing that matters is Me, Myself and I. But as I often say, if you want to go fast, go alone but if you want to go far, go together.

There is a saying used in training; ask someone how to spell the word 'team' and you will be told:

- there is no 'I' in T.E.A.M.

- T.E.A.M. means Together Everyone Achieves More.

Those sayings would have been lost on Susan, who once famously announced in a training session that she saw herself as a team of 'one' because that's how good she felt she was at her job. Unsurprisingly, things progressively got worse, to the point where one team member who was pretty fed up with Susan cut out the words from one of the store's advertisements, put double-sided tape on the back and placed it gently on the back of Susan's jacket. Susan spent an hour or so ignorant of the fact that she was walking around the store with a sign on her back announcing to the world that she was 'Hopelessly devoted to herself'.

At this point I was brought in to coach the team. The key was to break the flow of negative synergy – get them to delete and dump all those negative thoughts and attitudes – and get them to understand that working as a team made them stronger. It worked (though I had to use quite a bit of WIIFM).

Command: Mute

When I present my 'mind computer' strategy at conferences many people identify with it, particularly those in the audience who have been replaying negative influences for far too long (like watching daily reruns of a depressing film). Alternatively they have had their positivity diluted by spending too much time with someone who has a pessimistic approach to life. In a work context this kind of person will say things like:

- 'Oh business is dreadful; we've never been so quiet.'

- 'We will never hit this sales target.'

- 'I think head office must have had too much vino when they planned these sales targets.'

When I role-play these comments (complete with the appropriate whingeing tone) on stage at conferences the entire audience laughs out loud because although the words may not always be the same, everyone knows someone like this. And many times people have said quietly to me, 'What you just did, that was me, I'm that negative moaner. I hadn't realised it until now but I'm going to stop this minute...' It's another light-bulb moment in the Mind Makeover!

You're bound to know someone like this, at work or at home, who constantly bemoans life. Beware, their energy is toxic. I think of such people as a Negative Nellie or a Negative Neil (apologies to all the Nellies and Neils out there – it's nothing personal, just a simple way to bring negative people to mind). How much does this person's negativity drag you down? Would you like to stop having negative feel-bad chats with Nellie or Neil? I bet you would!

So what are you going to do when they walk over to you for a chat? Even if they're simply a work colleague rather than a friend or family member, you can't leap up and shout 'Stop, don't come any nearer. I think I'm allergic to your toxic energy.'

Here's how to deal with your Negative Nellie or Neil and come away with your positivity intact. Mute the sound. Think of your mind as a computer and literally mute the sound. When anyone negative begins to share their depressing thoughts and opinions with you and before this dramatically changes your positive mood and makes you feel miserable, immediately press the Mute command inside your head.

I've practised this for years and it really works. A Negative Nellie or Neil can chat away and I hear the sound of their voice but I do not listen to what they are telling me. I choose only to hear – rather than *absorb* – what they are saying so that I do not assimilate their negativity or depressing outlooks on the economy, life, health, wealth, relationships or whatever else is wrong for them. Their negative views and energy are theirs alone and have no place in my day. I make good use of continuity noises like 'um', 'really', 'oh' and we get along nicely! Their views will not and do not create my world. That's solely my responsibility.

Command: Review & Edit

Make sure you consciously use all your mind computer commands, especially the Review & Edit command as it can either help or hinder you.

At times in your life it is beneficial to review a situation that didn't go exactly to plan and edit the experience. Essentially this means that you take what you have learnt from it so it will support you in the future. Explore whether there are things you would do differently next time. When you focus on what you have learnt from a situation in your life that didn't turn out as you expected, you will attract back to you solutions, positive energy, opportunities and improved forward plans.

I'm telling you to look back at experiences that didn't go to plan or that you regard as 'a failure'; things that you can learn from. If you regard something as 'a failure' you have a choice; you can either delete and dump it if you want to just let it go (as long as you can do this and it will not keep popping up in your thoughts), or I suggest you review and edit it. Thinking 'It was a failure' presses the STOP button in your life, and creates negative feelings and feedback. Instead, you need to focus on the positives you can take from all experiences and these will come easily when you review and learn. You need to live in the solution (future), not the problem (past). A bend in the road (of life) is not the end of the road as long as you keep going and navigate the bend.

For example, if you go for an interview and then receive a rejection letter you could delete and dump the experience, but wouldn't it just resurface the next time you went for an interview? You'll grow by doing a 'review & edit': what did you learn and what will you do differently next time? You may decide to prepare more, research the company in more depth, use the techniques you've learnt so far in the Mind Makeover and incorporate these into your planning and performance to put you in a peak state of confidence.

Positive thinking is reacting positively to negative situations. You will be doing this when you chose to pull out lessons learnt.

EXERCISE

Review & Edit

- Write down three past experiences that you view negatively, do not want to repeat and wish to improve upon next time.

- For each experience write down what you have learnt and would change about your attitude.

- For each experience write down what you have learnt and would change about your actions.

- Now edit this experience but play it back in your mind as you expect it will go for you next time. See your changed thinking, emotions and actions – role-play a successful outcome. (Repeat this a few times and make sure you File & Save this experience.)

■ What have you now learnt to enable you to file this as a positive learning experience or able to delete and dump the experience for good?

So to recap:

- **File & Save:** this is where you store all your positive, empowering, feel-good experiences.

- **Delete & Dump:** use to remove forever all the rubbish and 'feel-good' diluters you do not want to keep.

- **Mute:** switches off all sound when you do not want to absorb negative chat.

- **Review & Edit:** replay at any time you choose your personal experiences to take positive points and learn from, to improve similar experiences in the future.

Form the habit of asking yourself daily: attitudes are contagious … are mine worth catching? Your attitudes will be worth catching if you consciously File & Save, Delete & Dump, Mute and Review & Edit. This will help and support you to feel happier and more successful and fulfilled. Will it take effort? Yes. Is it worth it? Absolutely and your gain will be a hundred times more than your effort and input.

In the next chapter I'll share with you how to create phenomenal experiences by breaking through the boundaries of what you do now. If we each do what we are truly capable of, we will astound ourselves. We've no time to lose.

chapter seven

SMASH OUT OF YOUR COMFORT ZONE

In my experience, smashing out of your comfort zone and your habitual way of doing things leads to increased levels of success, happiness and fulfilment. It has worked for thousands of individuals that I've coached and, as a consequence, has generated millions of pounds in additional sales for the companies they work for.

By smashing out of their comfort zones, many of the people I work with soar to phenomenal new levels of personal commitment and hit all-time highs in personal performance. I've witnessed it so many times – and you could achieve the same with your Mind Makeover.

LIFE BEYOND THE JAR

Here is a revealing illustration of why staying within our comfort zones is very easy – but so limiting. In a fascinating experiment, a scientist placed flies in a jar and restricted their freedom in order to test if the flies had a 'comfort zone'. The flies were first placed in an open jar and, as you would expect, they kept flying out and escaping. They were then placed in a ventilated jar with a lid and left for a day. The lid was then replaced by a screen, which meant the flies had the full effect of air, as opposed to ventilation, but were still unable to escape the jar. Finally, the scientist removed the screen to let the flies escape. But a very strange thing happened. None of the flies tried to reach for the top of the jar and escape. The flies wouldn't even spread their wings. Not one.

The scientist was shocked. Why would the flies stay in the jar? The reason is simple. Because they no longer believed they could escape. Staying within the confines of the jar had become habitual and, as they had tried many times to escape over the course of one day (when the lid was firmly on), they simply stopped trying and gave up. The jar had become their entire world. It had become safe – their own little comfort zone.

Has this made you think about your comfort zone and stirred some motivational thoughts? I hope so.

CHOOSE YOUR PERSPECTIVE

For a minute, think about when you were a child. Each day was a new adventure packed with exciting things to do. Just imagine how many new things you did as a child each and every day. For children, each day is an opportunity to learn and the more new things they experience the better the day.

Would you say that young children each and every day smash out of their comfort zones? Absolutely. From the minute they wake, children are bursting with energy, enthusiasm and wonder. They unconditionally embrace the day ahead, the adventures it will bring and the unknown. For a child, the possibilities are exhilarating and exciting. Wouldn't it be fabulous if we could say the same? It is possible if you start to see things more from a child's perspective.

LAUGHTER IS THE BEST MEDICINE

Here's another thought to consider: how many times per day on average does a young child laugh? Researchers say the answer is over three hundred times. So how many times per day do you think the average adult laughs? Between six and eight times. Of course, there's no such thing as an average adult, but if you think of the people around you, you'll probably agree that the figure seems about right. Isn't it obvious that many of us are missing out on the enthusiasm, passion and commitment to grab each and every day with the force and intensity of a young child?

Now, ask yourself the following question: 'When was the last time I did something for the very first time?'

I ask this in the hope that the feelings it evokes will inspire you to try something new and outside your comfort zone – because life becomes more exciting when you jump out of that zone.

TIME FOR A EUREKA MOMENT

I have asked thousands of delegates at conferences when they last did something for the first time and at least 90 per cent of my audiences experience a powerful emotional response to the question. For many people this simple question triggers emotions that kick-start the journey of change. This is the light-bulb moment, where they go from total darkness to seeing a new way ahead. I want you to feel that same motivation to smash out of your comfort zone; to feel that not doing it is not an option. But take note. I can think of numerous times when I've been told by a delegate something along these lines: 'I haven't pushed out of my comfort zone for years and I'm now so highly motivated I want to do a runner from my life as it is now.'

And my reply? 'Lock all the doors, we have a life runner!' In a few seconds they have seen their life flash by and they decide to pack everything in and escape to an atoll in the Maldives, open a restaurant on a Greek island, something, anything to get away. STOP! This is not a *Shirley Valentine* moment here where you cut all ties and run away. Yes, I want you to smash out of your comfort zone but this is not about escapism – it's about pushing the boundaries, not running away.

I want you to smash the comfort zones in all areas of life, in your:

- beliefs

- expectations

- attitude and thinking

- feelings of self-worth and confidence

- aspirations and goals

- joy and happiness.

This strategy can affect your personal aspirations and performance in the key areas of your life: career, relationships, personal well-being, finances, travel and hobbies. It can also create a deep desire and motivation to add new vision and passion to what you do and how you do it.

Many people have told me that attending a Mind Makeover presentation was the catalyst for them to take massive personal action, which is very different from running away. Massive personal action results in massive personal changes. (I often use the word 'massive' because positive change should feel massive. Try it out. It's empowering when you do.)

Here are some of the things my Makeover clients have said:

- 'I'm now going to stop always talking about emigrating to Australia and I'm going to do it.' She did too as a single mum with two young children in tow and has since created a wonderful life for the three of them.

- 'I'm going to train as a florist; it's all I ever wanted to do. I was pushed into what I do now by my parents and I hate it.'

- 'I have put up with my whinging, complaining husband for years. He's got to go!' (I felt a surge of responsibility here and so I got her to agree that she would give it a month and try to coach him out of the apathetic state she believed he lived in.)

- 'I'm going to qualify as a scuba diver and book my first scuba holiday.'

So what does this inspire you to think of doing?

For many of us, motivation and inspiration only come when we are pushed off a 'life cliff', such as going through a divorce or being made redundant. Such experiences can be incredibly motivating. But why wait? We can become focused, energised and passionate to make what isn't working work – now! Think of the infuriating scenario where someone tells their partner they're thinking of leaving them because things aren't working out and they've become lazy and apathetic and upon hearing this news, hey presto, this person immediately wants to wine and dine them three times a week, join a gym, travel to interesting places with them and join them at their Latin dancing classes where, God forbid, they might meet another life partner who isn't apathetic! What are you thinking? Right – they're too damn late!

SO WILL YOU JUMP OR WILL YOU BE PUSHED OUT OF YOUR COMFORT ZONE?

What's it to be? My experience is that many adults do not jump out of their comfort zone easily or by choice. Most have to be pushed out of habitual ways of doing and being.

Would you say the same is true for young children?

Would you say that, like adults, most young children prefer *not* to venture out of their comfort zone and would rather do the same things over and over again without improving, growing, learning, exploring? I'm sure you will agree that this is absolutely *not* true. And we would be hard pushed to find a child who would want to repeat the same levels of performance day in day out for years at a time and live their life with the mind-set that many adults live by.

There is an obvious point to remember here. We were all once children and therefore the odds are that we also laughed hundreds of times a day, woke up excited about the day ahead and, every day, smashed out of our comfort zone. So – if we adopt the persona of the children we once were – we can choose to travel through our lives with grace, ease and humour. We can choose to love life and see it as a joyous and blessed journey, as opposed to little more than a survival exercise where we live in fear of the unknown and are plagued by tension, anxiety and worry.

Embrace the unknown

It's interesting how many adults lose their ability to be excited by unfamiliar territory and so replace feelings of excitement with fear. They become apprehensive about the unexplored and shy away from new ways of being and doing. It is said that at the top of the list of 'things that stress adults' are ambiguity, the unknown and the unfamiliar.

As an adult, being fearful of the unknown stops you releasing your full potential and taking risks; to feel the thrill of doing something new. Why? Because…

> *Your life truly begins the moment you jump out of your comfort zone.*

Now before you go all 'That's all very well for you to say...' on me, I appreciate that life as an adult is very different to life as a child, when there's so much more to experience for the first time and no real responsibilities and commitments.

Yet, please think about these questions:

- How come I laughed hundreds of times a day when I was a child and now I only laugh _____ times? (Only you can fill in the gap here.)

- Does the learning curve I was on as a child stop abruptly just because I've grown into an adult?

You deserve to have a vital focus in your life and to live it with fun and passionate enthusiasm. As your success coach I am asking you these questions for one reason only: to inspire and challenge you to want to do something new and take action; to want to jump out of your comfort zone and embrace new ways of thinking and living so that you can be all you are capable of being; to be the best you can be.

> ❝ Decide you want it more than you
> are afraid of it ❞
>
> **BILL COSBY**

Fear of the unknown dissipates with action. It's helpful to stop and review times in the past when you came out of your comfort zone in areas of your life and it felt thrilling. You did something for the first time and your confidence and passion for life soared.

EXERCISE

Previous experiences of smashing out of your comfort zone

I know there will be some!

- Write down three examples of when you smashed out of your comfort zone and it felt thrilling:

  In your career
  In your relationships
  In your hobbies.

- What did you get back and how did you feel?

- Did the thrill outweigh the initial feelings of ambiguity and uncertainty, and maybe fear? I know you will have answered yes to this one.

EXERCISE

What do you see?

Here's an exercise I've used with many people I've worked with. First copy the nine dots shown below onto a piece of paper, exactly as they are shown here:

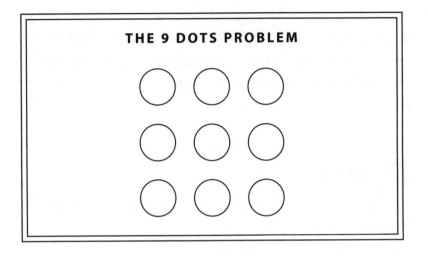

Once you've done this:

- using four straight lines, go through each dot in one continuous movement without taking your pen off the paper.

Imagine an audience of one hundred delegates. This is the outcome ninety-nine people out of one hundred get. Is it the same as yours?

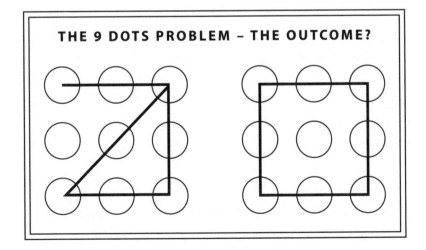

Picture those ninety-nine delegates believing this can't be done, there's one dot left, it's impossible. Imagine the energy force of ninety-nine individuals believing with absolute certainty that I'm wrong. It's powerful stuff I can tell you, when there are ninety-nine voices to one!

However, even if you are just one voice against ninety-nine, when you have faith – and not fear – and the secure knowledge and belief that it can be done then your one voice and energy will see you through.

Now look at the actual solution:

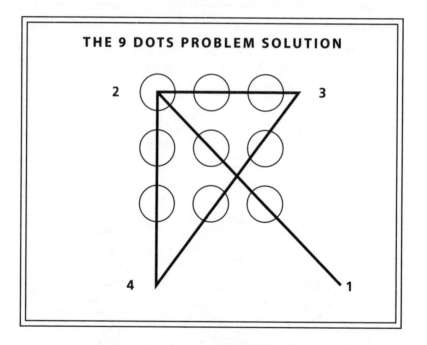

THE 9 DOTS PROBLEM SOLUTION

Here's what I shared with all those people who thought it was impossible.

- Line 1 – where did I begin? Yes, outside the box

- Line 2 – starts inside the box but finishes outside it

- Line 3 – starts outside the box (it's working so let's repeat it)

- Line 4 – yes, you've guessed it, outside the box.

So, who said it had to be done within the shape and confines of a box? I didn't. All I did was give the delegates the freedom to choose how they approached this exercise themselves; just as I gave you.

Be honest with yourself. Did you think within the box or did you think outside of it? If you did think outside the box you're in a very small minority. Most see a box and it doesn't occur to them to think outside the confines of it. The exercise is merely a metaphor for life and how you choose to live yours.

THINK OUTSIDE THE BOX

When doing the exercise above the majority of delegates see a box and, because of their habitual way of thinking, they play safe and stay within its confines. It does not occur to them to see it as anything other than a square box. They keep their thinking boxed in and, as a result, restrict their creativity, possibilities, opportunities and solutions. They see the task as something that 'can't' be done and 'impossible'. These two words are only a perception of the task in hand, not reality. Remember these two statements from the beginning of the book:

- If you always do what you have always done then you will always get what you have always got.

- Hell starts when the person you are meets the person you could have been.

Is staying where you are enough for you? Do you want to remain stuck in your comfort zone or do you want to feel the exhilaration of planning and doing something new? Wouldn't it be great to feel stretched and challenged and experience the euphoria of feeling and saying to yourself 'I did that, I pulled it off!'

Next time you are faced with an important task, opportunity or decision, outside your comfort zone, try this:

- think first before taking action – now that's novel!

- question, probe, analyse – maybe the answer you want is in the question you are going to ask

- be creative and think creatively of opportunities and solutions

- decide to take action now.

Once your mind is stretched it never goes back to its original size. Thank goodness!

EXERCISE

Examine your habits

Think deeply about the following question.

■ What are your personal comfort zones?

By this I mean where are you stuck in habitual ways of behaving and have kept your actions tightly within your comfort zone? Think of repetitive actions and restricted opportunities. I want you to consider whatever is working against you, diluting you and stopping you living to your full potential.

Think about your personal comfort zones in your:

1. career

2. relationships – work, social, family

3. hobbies

4. holidays

5. health and well-being

6. fitness

7. financial well-being

8. any other area.

Your aim is to expose whether your habits (habitual ways of being and acting in your life) are helping or hindering you; and are enhancing or diluting your success and happiness. Are they giving you your best life yet?

Ask yourself the following questions for each area of your life to clarify your self-awareness and write down your answers:

- Do I continually stay safely within my comfort zone or do I step outside it frequently and happily?

- If I am continually living my life staying within my comfort zone, then what impact does that have on my life?

- How and where does it restrict me and dilute my full potential and how does it stop me being the best I can be?

- If I decide now to continually live my life stepping outside my comfort zone, what impact would that have on my life?

- How and where would it empower me, enhance my potential and make me my best 'me' yet?

EXERCISE

Examine your thinking

Now list five areas where you feel you have got stuck in habitual ways of thinking; where you limit your thoughts of what is possible within your comfort zone? For example, if someone thinks, 'I simply adore ballroom dancing but it's something to learn when you're young', they're stuck in a comfort zone. A great friend of mine started ballroom lessons when she was fifty-three and four years later she's at competition standard and dancing is one of her greatest achievements and joys.

Remember, life truly begins when you take a leap and jump outside your comfort zone. To stay motivated by this empowering strategy, keep asking yourself the question:

When was the last time I did something for the first time?

Wouldn't it be tremendous if you could answer this question in the following way: 'The last time I did something for the first time was yesterday, or this morning, or an hour ago ...'?

Think again of the very first time you were asked this question or the first time you read it in this book. How did you feel? What emotions did it evoke? Did you feel either of the following?

■ Inspired because you continually do new things and seize new opportunities and, if there aren't any, you go out and create them.

■ Desperate because by asking yourself the question you realised that you rarely or never do new things and life has become too repetitive and habitual. You can't remember the last time you felt an adrenaline rush because you were pushing yourself to go beyond anything you have already mastered.

If it's the latter then you will know what you need to do by the end of the book.

WHAT MOTIVATES YOU?

Here's a poem that's made me smile and kept me mega-
motivated for years. I made a few tweaks and have kept a
copy ever since. It motivates me to get up early every day
and do an aerobics workout on my mini trampoline (not
always a good look but it works!)

> She's fat and she's wearing your clothes
>
> She's turning older than her years
>
> She's got too comfortable
>
> She was born on your birthday and at exactly the
> same time as you
>
> You're afraid that if you stop running she will catch
> up with you
>
> She's your shadow!

Here's a personal story that shows the joy you can have
when you step out of your comfort zone – and what better
motivator than joy!

I was the only person in my family who was qualified
to scuba dive and I decided that as a family it would be a
great way for us to come out of our comfort zone and do
something new together for the first time. My niece was
about to turn ten years old in January so I bought a special
Christmas present for her, my sister and my nephew: a
place on an eight-week scuba diving training programme,
every Sunday.

The present was received with a mix of emotions. There were screams of excitement from my niece and nephew but a 'I cannot believe you've done this to me' look from my sister, who was imagining eight Sundays of lessons and an exam to pass at the end. When I said, 'Annie, no pain no gain', I thought she was going to thump me. I softened the blow with bribery (it works every time): to celebrate we were all going to Egypt for a week in April, fully scuba qualified.

Now fast forward to April and our scuba holiday arrived. I will never forget our first dive. My niece was a very petite ten-year-old and the oxygen tank on her back was only a couple of inches shorter than she was. Other guests watched in horror as she launched herself into the water with total confidence and disappeared beneath the waves with her instructor.

During our first dive, we were in awe of the incredible beauty of the ocean. There was one magical moment when we were all moving along the seabed in a line, holding hands and letting the current move us along, when a giant turtle appeared and gracefully led the way. We followed the turtle for maybe five minutes – it was pure joy and emotional beyond words. As we got back onto the scuba boat, my sister, with tears in her eyes, said, 'That experience will stay with me for the rest of my life. It was truly a life experience and one to treasure forever.'

Memories this great are created by jumping out of your comfort zone and experiencing the thrill and adrenaline of doing something for the very first time. Try it once and you'll never look back. It's an addictive feeling.

NOW IT'S YOUR TURN

In the next exercise, I want you to think of three things you can do, would love to do and that you can start now. Before you begin, here is a tip. Do not think as most adults think. Instead, think like a child, and remember you were one once. Try to reconnect with the imagination and belief you had as a child. Bring it back into existence for this one exercise. Who knows, you may love how it feels to view the infinite possibilities of your unlimited potential through the eyes of a child. Think how fabulous life would be then.

Imagine a child completing this exercise and answering with total belief and passion, 'I want to go to Disneyland California and go on all the rides.' This is a great answer by a child. It smashes out of the comfort zone, creating a new experience and high.

But if you have children, an adult voice is probably saying 'Disneyland California? You must be kidding. How do you think I'm going to afford that? Are you nuts!?'

Be aware. Be very aware because a self-fulfilling prophecy such as this kicks in easily and negative thinking will not provide you with positive energy, ideas, solutions and imagination. Stop any 'I can't' thinking right now.

EXERCISE

Catapult yourself to new experiences

List three things you can do, would love to do and that you can start to do now.

One year from now, three years from now, five years from now ... you will be more disappointed by the things you did not do, than by the things you did do. So, wouldn't now be a good time to start and make your life experiences going forward truly memorable? Smash out of your comfort zone and feel the thrill of doing something for the first time.

I have seen so many people experience life-changing shifts in how they think and feel and as a consequence life-changing shifts in what they achieve. Success is not a destination. It is always a journey. Life is always evolving and you and I are in a world of continual growth. If you agree that life is growth then you must also agree that with growth comes change, continual change. So, instead of being fearful of change and the unknown, embrace change and make it work for, not against, you. Smashing out of your comfort zone is change and that is all it is.

> *Life itself is constant change so embrace it. Let change be your friend and not your enemy.*

Remember, if you don't like something change it, and if you cannot change it then change the way you think about it.

I love the serenity prayer:

Grant me the strength to accept the things I cannot change
The courage to change the things I can
And the wisdom to know the difference.

Decide right now to break out of your comfort zone because it feels fabulous when you do.

STUCK IN A RUT? THE SIGNS

It's now time to pull all this together and revisit the story at the beginning of the chapter; the one with the flies in a jar. Let's make this story really personal to you – have you been circling around the tight perimeters of your jar for way too long? Have your actions, performance and personal behaviour been habitual for too long?

You may have taken some small, safe trips beyond your known world; popped your big toe outside your comfort zone (but only your big toe, no more than that). Truthfully, hand on heart, were they all mini experiences and journeys into fairly familiar territory and all with an easy, quick retreat back to life as you know it?

You know you are or have been stuck in the jar when:

- nothing has felt thrilling and new for you for as long as you can remember

- it's been a long time since you felt the thrill of knowing you are committed, with no easy way out – you have to pull it off and not doing it is simply not an option

- all the things you dream about – when 'X' happens, if 'Y' happens then I'll travel, learn to salsa, get the dream job, volunteer, etc. – are simply daydreams

- you have had the same daydreams for years

- even those who love you look bored when, once again, you start talking about your daydreams for next year at the New Year celebration (particularly when it's mixed with alcohol and lots of excuses…)

- you feel bored and predictable most of the time.

If you relate to any of this then give your thoughts a Mind Makeover and get excited thinking about a 'break out' from the jar.

Try the following:

- Be creative. Think and focus on something that stirs your soul, gets your adrenaline pumping and gets you to wake up with positive energy and excitement for the day ahead.

- Aim to feel as excited as a child. For a child, the view from where they are standing is an exhilarating and exciting one, packed with new things to do and learn.

EXERCISE

Where do you want to go?

Think about these questions and write down the answers in your notebook:

- What would I do, have and be that I'm not yet?

- What would I change?

- What would I learn?

- How would I grow?

- Where would I improve?

- Where would I go?

- What could I do for the first time?

- How would I achieve it?

So you're now highly motivated to smash out of your comfort zone and journey into new, uncharted territory. How exciting for you.

> *Do something new, in this moment,*
> *in this day and you'll astound yourself.*
> *The biggest mistake you'll ever make is*
> *to be afraid of making one.*

Everyone is gifted but some choose never to open the package. Don't be one of them. Every day do at least one thing outside your comfort zone. You'll be amazed at the results you get and the positive emotions you experience.

The next chapter is packed with ideas on how to do this.

chapter eight

IMAGINE AND ASTOUND YOURSELF

Your imagination – your ability to positively visualise your future – is an amazing source of empowerment and has the potential to enrich your life immeasurably. Why? Your imagination can move you relentlessly towards your goals and your best life yet. And if you're thinking, 'Oh this creative stuff isn't for me, I can't imagine and visualise things', stop right there. That's a cop-out that will limit your success. We all have an imagination.

YOU'VE DONE THIS BEFORE

Imagination is innate within children. Remember when you were a child? In your early years you excelled at living in the world of your imagination. All children do. If an infant sees an empty cardboard box it becomes a ship to sit in and sail across the kitchen floor, a den, a monster's lair, a magic box...

Imagination is key to picturing your future in advance – you simply need to employ it. I've had some of the best times of my life in my imagination. Guess what? Most of these wonderful positive visualisations are now a reality. Trust me on this, using imagination and visualisation works.

However, there is a potential down side to using your imagination; one that many people fall victim to. People often use their spectacular imagination to picture negative things happening; they find worries and worst-case scenarios in everything. But if your constant companion is worry – those nagging 'What ifs', such as 'What if I fail?', 'What if it doesn't work?', 'What if I look ridiculous?' – then those worries will bounce back to you as your reality (those old thought boomerangs again). Some people do this. But not you, right?

> *Worry is a misuse of your imagination.*

Remember you have a choice. You can choose to use your imagination to help you turn your dreams into reality. It's your life and no one else's so what you choose to do is your decision. You can focus on your desires and goals or on your imagined worries. You'll prove yourself right either way.

Use your imagination correctly and it will help you to:

- identify where you want to go

- clarify your goals

- motivate you to step outside your comfort zone

- attract energy, ideas and opportunities

- increase your self-belief and confidence

- rehearse what you want to achieve (in a no-risk way)

- turn your dreams into reality.

Using your imagination gets you to think and feel your goals into existence. Top athletes, international sports teams and high achievers use this strategy to achieve optimum success. Why? Because they know their mental strength is as crucial as their physical strength and skill. It's a fact. Read about any top sports star and you will find that imagination and visualisation are critical to their training. Many athletes say that they won the game in their heads (in their imagination) before the game started. Think Olympics. In addition to training for four years, they play out winning in their imagination over and over again until winning feels real.

By now, you know your mind is neutral; it will not judge, assess and evaluate the information, focus and thoughts you choose to feed into it. It will just accept what you give it. So use this to maximum advantage to enable you to fast-track towards what you want to have, be and do in your life.

Let's start with thinking of one big goal you would like to achieve. What would be the dominant vision that would come to mind if I asked you what one thing you really want to achieve or do? Now carry out the following exercise.

EXERCISE

Imagine your goal as a reality

- Decide on that big goal and vision. As an example, I've seen people use their imagination to:

  - start their own business

  - plan their world travels

  - get a new job

  - learn how to speak to a large audience

  - get promoted

  - run a marathon

  - find their dream home.

- Clear the clutter out of your mind. Park your daily 'to do' list.

- Now find a quiet space to still and focus your mind on your goal and vision.

- Picture yourself having already achieved your goal (the home, job, promotion, the trip of a lifetime, etc.). Use all your senses: as well as seeing it, imagine how it would feel and hear what it would sound like; make it so you can almost touch it because it's so very real to you. Make your picture bold, full colour and at high volume. Make it a moving picture like a film.

- Play your goal out in your mind just as you would play a DVD on an enormous TV screen.

- Repeat this exercise a number of times until you've really got it fixed in your mind.

At the end of this chapter we'll consolidate this exercise so that it's really fixed in your mind.

This is your winning formula and will turn what you want into what you have now.

The Million Pound Club

The following story demonstrates the immense power of the imagination.

Several years ago I coached Sarah, the manager of a beauty counter in a department store. The cosmetics company she worked for had set a goal of achieving sales of £1 million in a single year, in two years' time.

At the start of her Mind Makeover programme Sarah confided in me that she was floundering and was daunted by the sales target she had been set. By the end of her four-day Mind Makeover session she'd had an enormous shift in attitude and told me, 'I know I can do it; my imagination kicked in, I can see it and it feels real. I'm going to hit the "million pound" goal a whole year earlier than the company thinks is possible. I've always had the potential to do it. The difference is that I now have total belief and faith in myself. I know I can do it!' I knew she could too.

Sarah used every ounce of her imagination. She pressed 'Mute' when others said it was too difficult, threw out the word 'impossible' and put her energies into her imagination, visualising hitting that sales target. She replayed it big and bright and lived it really happening many times every day in her imagination. Remember, using pure imagination will give you positive energy and inspirational 'out-of-the-box' ideas. And she got her entire team on board through her determination, passion, excitement, enthusiasm and ability to lead.

Four months later, my phone rang and when I heard the squeals of delight I knew immediately that it was Sarah, because it was the last day of the company's fiscal year. She'd just made the sale that had turned that £1m target into a reality. When she calmed down a little she said, 'You knew I could do it. Then once I got into the habit of visualising my success over and over again *I* knew I could do it. I had total belief.'

So where could total belief take you?

IMAGINE YOUR WAY THROUGH THE TOUGH TIMES

Your imagination is not only your greatest ally when focusing on the 'end product' – what you want to achieve. It is an important tool when you come up against obstacles that threaten to derail your plans.

Successful people are not without problems and obstacles; they simply view them as surmountable. They use their magnificent imagination to visualise solutions and see out-of-the-box ideas.

Try this for one week. Remove the word 'problem' from your vocabulary and replace it with the word 'challenge'. Thinking 'I have a problem' will trigger negative energy but saying 'I have a challenge' totally reframes what is happening, propels your thinking into the future and gives you back the positive energy to enable you to think through solutions and find opportunities. See obstacles and challenges as a positive part of the journey you are on to reach your goal. Challenges make life interesting and overcoming them makes you successful. They should stretch you not stop you.

When I was writing this book I was faced with some pretty large obstacles that could so easily have derailed the project. Rather than be dragged down by the problems I used my imagination to reinforce my vision of my goal, and overcome them: I imagined what the book would look like in my hands, in a bookshop window, being featured in a magazine, advertised in the press and so on. The more I imagined and played out in my mind the book being published, the more my life moved towards making it happen. I had lived it so many times in my imagination (big, bold and sensory) that I had complete faith and belief it would happen. And it did. Just as what you live in your imagination can and will materialise for you.

So keep visualising what you desire. Make it the predominant thought in your imagination and visualise it – using as many empowering scenarios as you need – with total belief and focus. Then, when challenges or setbacks occur, the energy and solutions to keep going will appear, because the law of attraction will create them.

IMAGINATION BOARDS

If you find it difficult to use your imagination – and even if you don't – imagination boards are a great way to really engage with your goal and 'see' what you are aiming for as clearly as possible. An imagination board allows you to take what you are visualising and make it tangible.

EXERCISE

Create an imagination board

The purpose of this exercise is to create a picture of what you desire.

- Keeping your goal in mind, look for pictures that, for you, represent that goal. These can be from magazines, brochures, promotional material from banks, articles written by people who have what you want – anything that visually represents your goal.

- Cut out the images, stick them on a board then put your board where you can easily see it. Look at it as many times each day as you can and you'll attract the positive energy and ideas you need to make it materialise in your world. You will succeed.

There's no need to stop at one – I have imagination boards all over the place. They're fun and they're a great way of bringing success into your life.

My first imagination board

Several years ago, my mum found an exercise book in a box in the loft. It was a project I did when I was ten. I can't remember doing it and it astonished me. Why? Because the project was an imagination board that mirrors exactly what I do now to visualise the things I want; to get them to materialise in my life.

The project included a piece called 'Looking into the future'. At ten years old I had designed the house I would live in, the furniture, my dining room (this had a stunning glass table and chairs to seat sixteen people – an odd choice for the woman who now makes dinner reservations more easily than she cooks). But the thing that took my breath away was a two-page spread showing my very own swimming pool. I didn't even know then that there were homes with their own swimming pools. My family visited the swimming baths at least once a week and my sister and I could swim before we could walk, but to have a pool at home where you lived just wasn't on the radar. Roll forward four decades and guess what? I have a swimming pool and I swim nearly every day.

Now that fact isn't included to impress you, simply to impress upon you that when you have a vision, see it bright and bold in your mind constantly and make an imagination board, then by the law of attraction you will get back the positive energy, ideas and opportunities to bring what you imagine into your world.

So maximise the power of your imagination; take action and start putting together that imagination board now!

Know without doubt that when you work with true passion and belief, with all you have for all you want, then what you want will be yours. Know absolutely that what you desire will become your reality.

USE NO-RISK REHEARSALS

Business high achievers rehearse what they want to achieve in their imagination. This is a particularly effective strategy for giving a successful presentation at a meeting or conference, but you can use it for any important event. You simply picture in your mind the meeting, presentation or important event; see it in your imagination, and in full colour, going brilliantly. See yourself achieving your objectives and getting positive feedback from others. Imagine it vividly and positively and repeat this as many times before the event as you can.

I've coached many executives to speak effectively in public (researchers tell us it is the second most common fear in the world). I get them to tap into how they will feel when they do the presentation and also how they will feel afterwards when they have done the job well and to the very best of their ability. I get them to see it and feel it many times. All that is then required is for them to learn the skills to present effectively, hold the attention of the audience and plan content to achieve objectives. Then and only then are they ready to go live. They can stand up on the day and deliver it brilliantly. The success they have imagined was just waiting for them to claim it, because confident people use their imagination to maximise their impact and potential.

Repetition of role-playing in the mind generates great outcomes. This could be you. Use your imagination to attract success to you. If it's worth doing, live it in your imagination first.

Try out your ideas and what you desire by imagining them in action first because using your imagination is like watching a pre-launch trailer for a fantastic film. The difference is this film is your life. Imagine yourself becoming and being the person you want to be. It's positive imagery – like a dress rehearsal. Picture your future in advance being all you want it to be – fabulous.

TURN UP THE VOLUME

Adding sound to your visualisation is a great way to make it stronger, so use this to your advantage. Choose music that fits with what you are visualising and that makes you feel empowered and inspired. And listen to it often, not only when you are actively visualising the outcome you want. When you listen to the music at any time it will trigger positive energy and thoughts of what you want to achieve, reinforcing those thought boomerangs.

While writing *The Mind Makeover* I listened to one of my favourite songs, 'Pure Imagination', from the film *Charlie and the Chocolate Factory* (search for the words online – they're very uplifting). I began each day listening to the words as I focused on the immense power of my imagination, adding a sensory dimension that made the publication of the book even more real to me.

You will find more on the subject of music and visualisation in Chapter 10.

BECOME A POSSIBILITY THINKER

Decide to be a possibility thinker. This means that you consciously choose to think thoughts that are full of possibility. Use positive 'What ifs' and replay the end result many times. For example, what if I…?

- excel at the company conference when I present
- learn to ski
- reach my ideal weight
- live in a different country
- land my dream job
- meet my perfect partner
- buy my own home

Remember, you can think 'I can' and you can also think 'I can't'. Guess what, either way you're right! Let your imagination empower and enhance your life, not dilute it. Think 'What can I do?' and 'What's possible?'

WHAT ABOUT THE MANY THINGS YOU 'DON'T HAVE YET'?

At this stage in your Mind Makeover you are a person who is a positive, glass half-full, optimistic type. Simply said, you are fabulous! You're someone who focuses on what's right in your world. But if you choose to try and live your best life yet this will inevitably highlight all the things that you want in your life but don't have yet.

> *Reality can be beaten with even*
> *a little imagination.*

In the last chapter I shared the dangers of focusing your attention on what you believe you 'can't do' or 'don't have' as this triggers negative emotions and will become a self-fulfilling prophecy. But you can use 'don't haves' to your advantage. Here's how. You can chose to use your imagination to positively reframe and picture things you don't have yet (but want). Reframe them as your goals. Be clear about what it is you want and play the film in your imagination bold and loud. Hold that thought vividly and often and you will attract what you need to you.

> *When you hold it in your mind*
> *you will hold it in your life.*

EXERCISE

Bring your desires into existence

Positively, think of the things you'd like in your life:

- the person you will be with (if you're not with that person already)

- the career and job you will have (if you're not in that job already)

- the home you will live in (if you're not living in that home already)

- the places you will travel to and the new things you will learn (scuba diving, languages, salsa dancing?)

- the money you will have (earnings and savings).

The list is endless and it is *your* list.

Keep your thoughts and list close to you at all times, and make them your prominent focus. Be consistent in your thoughts so that opportunities, ideas and things you desire will evolve for you and be available for you to act upon. Thinking empowering thoughts will generate the right energy source to create and attract your desired life, working as a magnet to your thought boomerangs.

THE BEST WAY TO PREDICT YOUR FUTURE

The best way to predict your future is to create it. And the only place to create it is in your magnificent mind and imagination! When you decide to vividly live something in your imagination it will materialise in your world for you to live it.

Here is the really big question of this chapter: What is it you dream of and desire? Imagine it now. Think and feel it into existence.

EXERCISE

Your imagination – use it or lose it

1. What is the number one goal you want to live out in your imagination? Look back to the exercise on page 175. Do you have the same goal or have you stretched your imagination to another goal?

2. Describe it. How do you picture it, visualise it? How will you role-play it in your imagination and mind?

3. What will you put onto your imagination board for this one goal?

4. What music would you add to turn up the volume on your goal?

5. How will you feel when you achieve your goal and your dream becomes your reality? What emotions will you experience?

Fail to plan and you plan to fail

Now that you know your goal and have visualised it many times you need a plan of action. What ideas and visions have your imagination and thoughts given you to turn what you want into a reality? What actions do you now need to take? The indispensable first step to getting what you want out of life is this: simply decide what you want.

EXERCISE

Goal planning

- Write down your one big goal and make it SMART (Specific, Measurable, Ambitious, Realistic, Timed). It's a dream until you write it down and then it becomes a goal.

It must be specific and measurable to get maximum results. A client told me his goal was to have more money. To which I opened my wallet and gave him a one pound coin. He didn't say how much he wanted! He got the point and was never vague about his goals again. Be ambitious. Be realistic in your timing and set yourself up to win. Give your goal a deadline or it will roll on year after year.

- Now write a list of every single action you can think of and imagine that will get you to achieve your goal. Break your actions down as small as possible. If you leave your 'to do's' too big in size and time you will not fit them easily into your diary (and that's part of the plan). Write fast, think fast and don't worry about the order.

- Take your list and re-write it in a logical order in your diary or computer diary.

- Assign an appropriate date to every task. (Write each task that is in your goal to-do list in a different colour so it jumps off the page.)

- Commit to ticking off every action on your list on the exact day it is written in your diary, starting now!

Goal planning is pivotal in moving you from where you are now to where you want to be. Organising a wedding is the perfect example of how essential goal planning is. On a set day at a set time so many different elements need to be in place: the dresses, food, transport, flowers, music, photography, guests (oh and the groom!)… And how is it achieved? By using exactly the same strategy for goal planning as I've shared here and breaking the goal down into all the actions that need to be taken, writing a to-do list and doing it in the right order. It's a technique that can be applied to every day of our life. I know it works because I've seen thousands achieve ambitious goals, and so does Sarah who hit her £1 million sales target on the exact day she planned to. I've also yet to hear of a bride who did not achieve her goal and arrived at the church without having bought a wedding dress, all because she didn't make a plan.

You now have all you need to explore and dive into the magical world that is your imagination. So go and buy that board, start cutting out pictures and turn the music on. There's no better time to begin moving towards your goal. The world of your imagination is a magical place to go. Allow it to work its magic for you.

chapter nine

YOUR INNER VOICE

What do you say when you talk to yourself? It's time to be honest here. We all have an inner voice and, whether we admit to it or not, we all hold conversations with ourselves. Sometimes you will be conscious of your inner voice chatting away and at other times you will be completely unaware of it.

Is this inner voice, or 'self-talk', a good or a bad thing? The answer depends on what you are telling yourself. Are you telling yourself that your life is full of good things and opportunities, and that you're fabulous and talented? Or are you telling yourself the opposite?

You can change and also stop a negative inner voice just as you can stop a bad habit. This chapter will show you how.

Before we begin it's vital to remember that:

> 6 The most important opinion is the one
> you have of yourself and the most significant
> things you say in your day are the things
> you say to yourself. 9
>
> ZIG ZIGLAR

GET TO KNOW YOUR INNER VOICE

I want you to connect with your inner voice. Become conscious of what that voice is telling you and, in particular, the specific words and statements it – that is, you! – use. Only then can you take charge of your self-talk.

Your inner voice will chat away to you about all areas of your life; there are no restricted areas. It will offer opinions about your well-being, aspirations, abilities, career, finances, relationships, education … The list of potential topics is endless.

Where does your inner voice come from?

Your inner voice stems mostly from what you were consistently told by adults in your childhood and formative years and also from the non-verbal messages you received. Of course, what we are told can be positive but it can also be very negative. Unfortunately, it is often the bad that is carried forward. For example, when a child repeatedly hears adults describe them as shy then guess what? Over time they grow to believe it. So guess how they react when their line manager at work asks them to talk in an important meeting?

I'll never forget the day I took my nephew to nursery and listened to one of the mums say to her daughter several times, 'Oh Charlotte, stop being so shy.' If I'd had this book then I would have willingly hit Charlotte's mum with it. As I didn't, she got a mini Mind Makeover on the consequence of what she was saying to poor Charlotte. She was not amused.

Your inner voice generates lots of different emotions. But, as I've said many times before, you always have a choice – and that choice also applies to what you say to yourself. And because you choose what to say, you also get to choose the emotions that arise as a consequence. Your self-talk will give you back feelings of either:

- confidence or anxiety

- faith or fear

- mediocrity or excellence

- a 'can do' or 'can't do' attitude

- fun or misery

- happiness or sadness

- excitement or frustration

- a sense of opportunities or limitations

- a desire to collaborate or conflict with others

- knowledge or ignorance

- kindness or bitterness

- hindrance or helpfulness

- passion or apathy.

Remember, when communicating with other people we do not always mean what we say or say what we mean. It is exactly the same with our inner voice. Often we don't have a clue what is going on 'in there' and just let our inner voice babble on.

In this chapter I will share all you need to get a strong and confident inner voice. But you must first know your start point: take time now to think back and reflect on your inner voice and I will ask you one simple question: is your inner voice and self-talk serving you well and empowering you or is it diluting your potential?

EXERCISE

What's your story?

Think of a personal example where you've allowed a negative inner voice to hold you back. Which area in your life stands out for you (bear in mind that it might be years old and on a continual repeat loop)? Give this some serious thought; it'll be worth it.

- What have you been saying to yourself?

- What was the consequence of this inner voice?

- What can you now change and turn it into a positive empowering message?

- ■ Stop this negative voice now. Review, change and reframe what your inner voice has told you about the event or experience (it may well be from your childhood and completely irrelevant). Better still, delete and dump it because no matter how attached you are to it, it does not enhance your life.

Your own radio station

Think of your inner voice like an internal radio station playing inside your head, with many different channels for you to select from. There's a channel to uplift and empower you, but be careful; there's also a channel to depress and dilute your happiness and potential success.

This is your radio and you choose what you want to listen to. Tune in and be aware of the channel and the chats you have with yourself inside your head. Are you switched on to the empowering or the depressing channel? Be sure to pick the right one as it triggers and creates your moods, beliefs, motivation and subsequent actions: in two simple words – your future.

YOUR INNER VOICE – ENEMY OR FRIEND?

Your words impact your thoughts, actions, outcomes and life, therefore your inner voice can be either a friend (a positive and empowering energy) or an enemy (a negative and diluting energy). Don't be your own worst enemy because:

> *It is hard to beat the enemy if its office is based inside your head.*

Sadly, many people go through their lives hand in hand with the enemy and fill their days with negative, harmful inner voices and self-talk.

Here are some of the things the enemy says:

- 'I can't do it'
- 'I haven't got the time, education or money to do it'
- 'I'm not clever enough'
- 'I'm too young/too old to do it'
- 'I've always been shy'
- 'I never lose weight; weight problems run in the family'
- 'I hate exercise'
- 'I'm lazy'
- 'I never feel passionate about anything'
- 'I just don't have the energy I used to have'
- 'There's no fun in anything anymore'
- 'I've gone as far as I can go in this job'
- 'I don't remember things well'
- 'Today's just going to be one of those days' (and it's only 9 a.m.!)

- 'I always meet losers'

- 'It must be me. It always happens to me'

- 'It's impossible'

Do any of these sound familiar? Bear in mind that if you expect to be disappointed you'll seldom disappoint yourself. Recognise and make a note of any that you say to yourself and delete them – they do not serve you, they dilute you and have no place in your life. Bin them.

Notice how many of the typical negative statements above involve absolutes like 'I always', 'I never'. They create a cycle in which words become actions and outcomes:

- I won't = you will never get started

- I can't = you will never try

- I can't be bothered = laziness will keep you stuck where you are

- I don't know how = so go and find out

- I wish I could = you're being 'a gonna' (never put a wishbone where your backbone should be)

- I think I might = you will hesitate

- I might = you will be indecisive

The good news is that you can change negative self-talk into positive self-talk. Don't allow your inner voice to tell you 'it's impossible'. Instead, tell yourself all things are possible if you desire them enough.

- I think I can = you're starting to believe

- I can because I have = power from reviewing past achievements

- I will = you are committed and motivated to act

- I have = congratulations and now you can repeat your success

- I did it = recognition of achievements and success

EXERCISE

What do you believe is possible?

What do you believe is now possible, that you once thought impossible? I want you to know with certainty you can delete the inner voice telling you something's 'impossible' and replace it with what is possible.

- Make a list of all the things you believed in before people sold you the story that they were impossible. For example, I can have enough money to live a fabulous life, I can lose all my extra weight, I can conquer my fear of flying, I can get a degree, I will meet someone really special.

- Now become a possibility thinker and make a list of all the things you were told and believed were impossible that you now know are not. For example, I can start my own business, I will do a round-the-world trip, I can take up running...

> *If you find yourself saying, 'It can't be done, it's impossible', stop and look around you. You will see someone doing it.*

Recently I was at a birthday party where the theme was *Alice in Wonderland* by Lewis Carroll. As I entered the party down a tunnel filled with fairy lights, a clip of Alice and the Queen was playing and the words had an instant impact:

> 'There's no use in trying,' said Alice. 'One cannot believe impossible things.' 'I daresay you haven't had much practice,' said the Queen. 'Why when I was your age, I always did it [believed the impossible] for at least half an hour a day. Why sometimes I believed as many as six impossible things before breakfast!'

It's a wonderful approach to life and it's yours to adopt *now*. Take away self-imposed limits. Change the word impossible to the word possible and watch things improve enormously. Move the boundaries you've agreed to as a result of listening to negative self-talk. Remember, negativity cannot survive without your participation and permission. Delete it.

Enemy inner voices will have a massive negative impact on your life. Think about it: you are actually telling yourself that you don't believe in yourself. You now know all about the 'law of attraction' so you know the negative impact this kind of thinking will have on you.

In short, never set yourself up to lose. Always set yourself up to win. Tell yourself daily that you are braver than you think, more capable than you know, stronger than you seem and smarter than you've been yet.

The mind is neutral; it will not judge, assess and evaluate the information and thoughts you choose to feed it. It just accepts them. How tremendous is that? This means you can choose whether you want your mind to accept either the perception or reality of what something is, as it makes no difference to your mind whether something is real or imagined.

Look at this picture, what do you see?

Do you see the musician ... or the lovely girl? Each image is as valid as the other. We all have a choice in what we decide to think and see in our minds, the pictures we form and what we choose to tell ourselves.

GUILT TRIPS – WHY GO ON THEM?

Does your inner voice and self-talk say things like:

- 'I must lose weight'

- 'I've got to get a better job'

- 'I have to spend more time with the kids [or family, friends…]'

- 'I should be a better daughter [mum, sister, friend…]'

- 'I ought to get fit'

- 'I've just got to save some money'?

When you say to yourself 'I ought to, I've got to, I have to and I should do', then what you are really saying to yourself is 'I can't do it' and also 'I don't do it and I should'. Quite simply, it's a vicious circle. Your whole focus is on what you have to do and not on what you want to do. This weighs you down with bucket-loads of guilt and is a stress trigger. Stop it *now*.

How to stop the guilt trip

Here's how to stop the guilt trip and turn a negative thought into a positive one that will empower you:

- 'I've got to lose weight.' Instead, say 'I want to lose weight' and focus on how you can.

- 'I must get a better job.' Instead, focus on and ask yourself, 'What are my talents and passions; what job would suit me best?'

- 'I'm too fat' or 'I'm too thin'. Instead, focus on and tell yourself, 'I'm great just as I am and I'm excited about making an even more fabulous version of me.'

- 'I'm so stupid.' Instead, focus on and tell yourself, 'So, I made a mistake; good, I'll learn from it.'

- 'I'm too old' or 'I'm too young'. Instead, focus on and tell yourself, 'Age is irrelevant. I'm not cheese.'

Choosing to focus on and put your energy into what you perceive is wrong, broken or lacking in your life will not get you anywhere you want to go. It will only add fuel to any doubts and fears. Don't sign up to be your own enemy. Change all your thinking and focus on what you do want and attract it to you. Decide to live in your future not the past; to focus on the solution not the problem and view your world with an 'I can' attitude.

Ditch negative and ambiguous words

These are the negative words and phrases to delete from your vocabulary:

- I can't

- But (this word is usually followed by an excuse)

- I have to (touch of martyrdom slipping in here)

- I won't

- Impossible

- If (beware – to my mind this stands for I.F., Instant Failure and is usually followed by an excuse).

Ambiguous words should also be ditched. I think of these as 'grey' words as they are hesitant and full of doubt:

- Maybe

- Possibly

- I'll try

- Should have, could have, would have.

Do not be ambiguous. Always be specific and focused.

Can or can't?

So which is it for you – can or can't? Whether you think you can do something or whether you think you can't, by the law of attraction you'll prove yourself right! So make sure you're always telling yourself 'Yes I can'.

You can decide to make changes immediately. Here's how to do it:

EXERCISE

Delete the negative

1. Expose all negative words and statements your inner voice says as it's chatting to you (enemy statements).

2. Use your mind computer to delete and dump them all. If it helps, write them down and then score through them.

Creating and maintaining self-belief is a life-long journey as well as part of your Mind Makeover; it's an on-going process. Only sign up to self-talk that allows you to love and respect yourself. Delete the rest. If at this point a little gremlin in you head is saying, 'But I'm not perfect!' I know! Neither am I – just aim to be a fabulous work in progress.

Now you have ditched the negative voices and statements, let's turn your inner voice into your supportive friend.

BE YOUR OWN BEST FRIEND

Use empowering supportive words

Here is a list of positive empowering words that should feature prominently in your vocabulary, both internal and spoken. Tell yourself:

- Yes

- I can

- I will

- I am

- I understand

- It's possible/definitely

- However, what if… (followed by a solution)

- I'm blessed I get to do (better than 'I have to do')

- I commit to

- I appreciate

- I plan to

- I've arranged for

- I've completed

- I achieved

- I learnt

- I decide to

- I choose to

- I focus on

- I'm proud of

Think back to Chapter 4, where we looked at the iceberg theory and the immense power of attitude. Always add a positive attitude and belief to the words you consciously select and use. Then, and only then, will the words you say be empowered with a positive tone and intonation and have a much greater impact. Your words must match your thoughts. For example; when you say 'I can do it', you must also see it, feel it and believe it for you to achieve it or for it to materialise in your world.

Learn new empowering statements

Imagine your inner voice saying things like:

- 'Everything I want is possible'

- 'I can lose weight'

- 'I will get a better job'

- 'I *want* to spend more time with the family'

- 'I'm blessed'

- 'I will get fit'

- 'I am in control of my destiny and dreams'

- 'I do a great job'

- 'I'm happy and fulfilled'

- 'I have complete belief that I can do this'

- 'I've put in the effort and I will excel at this'

- 'I love doing this'

- 'I'm spending my time on my priorities'

- 'I feel brilliant' (any happy, positive word is good here)

- 'I respect myself and the decisions I make'

- 'I'm proud that I take responsibility for my actions'

- 'I'm proud of myself and who I am'

- 'I have unwavering belief that this is possible'

- 'I'll stay positive and focused whenever I have challenges'

- 'I know I can find solutions to problems'

- 'I can because I have' (anything you have done even once before)

- 'I celebrate my fabulousness always'

- 'I live by putting all I have into all I want'

- 'I have more than enough time'

- 'I love my life'

- 'I believe in me'

- 'Talent and ability flow through me'

- 'I have everything I need in abundance'

Stop now and imagine if you approached each day of the rest of your life with this friendly inner voice speaking to you. The possibilities would be limitless and you would experience joy, happiness, success and fulfilment in abundance.

Now think back to Chapter 6, where I showed you how to use your mind like a computer: I want you to 'File & Save' all of the positive statements above and use them as daily self-talk to empower you. Learn them, use them and repeat them as often as possible. Where will they take you? Wherever you wish to go.

You are now in charge of your inner voice (when you choose to be). However there are two more words I want you to highlight as the enemy.

Two words you must delete

There are two words that have the power to stop you living your best life yet: failure and fear. Delete these two 'F' words from your vocabulary and:

- replace failure with learnt

- instead of fear have faith.

1. Failure

In life we all experience things that turn out as planned – and things that don't. The self-talk you choose to describe such experiences will dictate whether you gain from the experience or are diluted by it. Many people slip the word failure into their self-talk without realising it has an enormous negative impact.

Failure is not about falling down, it's about staying down. Failure is an attitude, an emotion, a way of thinking. It is not an end result (unless that is how you think about it and frame it in your world). When something does not work out as you expect or does not go to plan, this is not a failure. It is an opportunity to learn, be stretched, to adapt and make positive changes. Use what has happened to motivate you.

Take the story of Thomas Edison, the inventor of the light-bulb. Apparently he 'failed' hundreds of times. The story goes that a newspaper reporter asked him, 'How does it feel to have failed seven hundred times and still not have the answer?' Somewhat confused Thomas Edison replied, 'I haven't failed seven hundred times. Why would you ever think that? What I have done is succeeded in proving that these seven hundred attempts do not work … I have eliminated seven hundred approaches and once I have eliminated all the ways that will not work I will then find the one that will work.'

All ambitious activity – which is a necessary part of being happy, successful and fulfilled – brings with it adjustment, lessons learnt and experiences, not failures. So stop judging experiences in your life as either good or bad and simply see them for what they are, experiences to achieve and grow from, or learn, adapt and change from. Successful and fulfilled people are not people without problems. They are simply people who acknowledge problems for what they are – challenges to overcome – and manage them positively.

A charismatic company CEO I once coached was interviewed for a magazine article. One question was 'What has been your biggest business success?' The next question asked was 'What has been your biggest failure in business?' He replied, 'Failure? Let's see, I've never had any of those. Yes, I have done hundreds of things *once* that didn't work and I simply learnt very quickly not to do them that way again.' What would you go for if you knew with absolute certainty that you could not fail?

On a more personal level think about it this way: if something has not gone to plan (big time) for a close friend what would you tell them to do? Pick themselves up, learn from the experience and try again, or give up? It's obvious, isn't it? Always be your own friend.

So delete that 'F' word from your vocabulary *now*. It has no place in your life. Replace it with the word learn. With this one word substitution you have turned your inner voice from your enemy into your friend. Focus on your talents, passions and massive personal potential. It's all there waiting for you to tap into.

What worry gene?

Anyone I've coached in business who majors on 'Failures' is often a worrier. They have an inner voice saying: 'What if the worst happens?', 'What if I fail?', 'What if I look ridiculous and people laugh at me?' This kind of self-talk is soooo exhausting. Worry is a small thing that casts a big shadow, but if you are a worrier, take heart: in my experience as a success coach I've seen so many people throw away this bad habit and overcome their negative emotions.

Remember the success myth about the fairy godmother decreeing that some babies will be born lucky while others will not. Well the same applies to worry. Worriers are not born that way – a fairy godmother does not bestow a worry gene. And if you think that worry is a 21st-century emotion – forget it, it was depicted in ancient hieroglyphics. So don't blame our current lifestyles – we simply have different opportunities to worry from our ancestors.

Let me ask you: When you are in a state of constant worry, do the emotions generated by it kill off and strangle your positive energy, self-belief, confidence, ideas, passion, hope, creativity, happiness, success and sense of fulfilment?

Yes. I thought so. So wouldn't now be a good time to stop doing this and ditch the worry habit once and for all, because worry over small things casts a big shadow over your potential and is a misuse of your magnificent mind and imagination.

> ❝ I'm an old man who has known a great many problems, most of which never happened ❞
>
> **MARK TWAIN**

Worry – the facts

If you're not convinced, think about the following statistics. Research suggests:

- Approximately *40 per cent* of worries never materialise. So why waste your energy? Why not wait until something actually happens and deal with it then, rather than waste energy on what is essentially a figment of your imagination?

- Around *30 per cent* of worries are about the past. So don't look back. You cannot change what has happened. Worrying about it is emotionally draining and you gain precisely nothing.

- Around *22 per cent* of worries are small and petty. Our personal experiences are simply that, personal to us. They relate to all the areas of our life: our career, family, friends, relationships, etc. So can I suggest as your success coach that you be your very own 'best friend' for the entire journey, and focus on the important stuff?

So, from all those worries it would appear that only a small proportion of our worries materialise. Forget past problems and kick out petty and imagined worries – simply press Delete & Dump. When you do this you will feel empowered and in full control of your inner voice and self-talk.

When something difficult arises don't think of it as a 'worry'; replace the word 'worried' with 'concerned'. When you say 'I'm concerned' instead of 'I'm worried' it immeasurably alters your emotional state and focus for the better. 'Worry' is full of negative connotations, whereas 'concerned' activates positive energy and a desire to find a solution. Worry keeps you locked in the past whereas feeling concerned propels you into a future filled with solutions. So get to know what your real concerns are and the ones you *can* do something about. Be bold and deal with them full on. As the saying goes: live in the solution. It's worth remembering that if you don't like something then change it, and if you can't change it then change the way you feel about it.

Now, here's the second 'F' word to banish:

2. Fear

Allowing fear to become a part of your self-talk will stop you getting to where you want to go.

I've used the following mnemonic of the word FEAR for years:

- **False**

- **Evidence which**

- **Appears**

- **Real**

Banish the word 'fear' from your thinking and vocabulary right now. Let me ask you a question. Are you living with fear or faith? Both thoughts of fear and faith are boomerangs that will come back to you as emotional states and feelings. These emotions shape your actions – or lack of action.

> *Remember, the biggest mistake you'll ever make is being afraid to make one.*

Researchers tell us that public speaking is second on the list of what people fear most (number one is death). I use public speaking as an example often because at some time it comes to almost all of us, whether at work or in a social situation. Being fearful of speaking to an audience is no different to feeling fearful of asking for promotion or an increase in salary. Fear of taking action is only a way of thinking, an attitude. I want you to know how to face it, squash it and then do the very thing you were fearful of with confidence and self-belief.

Several years ago I coached public speaking skills to a senior executive called Julia, who had to make a presentation to an audience of over 500 colleagues. Be honest, how would you feel if you went to work tomorrow and you were asked to do the same? For Julia just the thought of having to stand and speak to a room of people, let alone a room of 500 people, filled her with overwhelming fear. Julia was *so* fearful of what she was being asked to do that she felt death for her might actually have been an easier option, and she'd also considered the thought that she might actually die if she did have to do it. I coached her on how to change her mind set, attitude, focus, thoughts and limiting beliefs – everything I'm sharing with you in *The Mind Makeover*, and I did this before I coached her on the techniques and skills required to present effectively.

Fast forward and after three weeks of coaching sessions, I sat in the audience at the company conference and watched Julia make her presentation with a level of confidence and ease that went beyond her wildest imagination and everyone in the audience applauded at the end. She described the experience to me as 'one of my greatest life moments'. Do you think this would have happened if she had allowed fear to stop her? No, absolutely not.

Initially fear did stop her and her first reaction was to resign, run like crazy and get another job. But she wanted to live life to her full potential so she stayed and faced her fears. She knew she could not live with herself if she copped out, resigned and went for a position that did not involve public speaking. And as far as I know, public speaking is not, and never has been, a cause of death.

> 6 The only limit to our realisation of tomorrow will be our doubts of today 9
>
> **FRANKLIN ROOSEVELT**

Be aware that when fear stops you once, you are on a habitual spiral of giving up when it gets tough.

EXERCISE

Old fears and doubts

To delete and throw out past fears that held you back you must first consciously expose and recognise them and become aware of the impact they have had on you. Only then will you feel confident enough to delete them and highly motivated to take the relevant action.

- List five old fears and doubts that have held you back. (These can be in any area of your life; career, relationships, hobbies, travels, etc.)

- Now write down the impact these had on you and how they made you feel.

I'm sure you don't want to experience these kinds of feelings again so let's look at how you can remove any doubts and replace fear with faith and positive belief.

Changing fear into faith

Here are the steps you need to take:

1. You have read above that at most times FEAR is false evidence which appears real. It is your perception of something and not the reality of it.

2. Face what you fear doing. Be bold.

3. Investigate and expose why you feel anxious and fearful. What's the reality? What is this based upon?

4. Ask yourself: Is it a lack of knowledge of 'how to do it'? Then go and get the knowledge.

5. Ask yourself: Is it based on negative self-talk? Delete it and change it to positive self-talk.

6. Ask yourself: Is it fear of doing it alone? Then build a support team. Connect to others doing similar things.

7. 'Self-talk' as many positive thoughts and statements as you can pack in.

8. Start to take action right now. Do one thing today to move you towards overcoming your fear.

9. Then continue to take massive action and make the necessary changes and shifts in your thinking each and every day.

> ❝ The journey of a thousand miles
> starts with a single step ❞
>
> LAO-TZU, CHINESE PHILOSOPHER

EXERCISE

Stop fear stopping you

What would you do if you knew you couldn't fail?

- Think of the future you want and ask yourself, if I were not afraid – if I had no fear of failing – what would I do and go for?

- Ask yourself: If I *don't* do this what will it cost me? What's the impact of not going for it? What will I miss out on? How would I feel?

- Ask: If I *do* go for this how will it benefit me? What's the impact of going for it? What will my reward be? How would I feel?

For most, *not* going for what they want (because they fear failure) ultimately costs them their self-esteem, pride and happiness. For most, *going* for what they want (and deleting inner voices telling them to be fearful of failing) gives them an abundance of motivation, happiness, success and fulfilment. It's an easy choice.

Think about the following – it's motivated me so many times to overcome fear and take the plunge:

> *Decide you want it more than you are*
> *afraid of it – whatever 'it' is for you.*

The greatest fear

As I pointed out before, for most the number one fear is death. Facing our mortality is a sure way to motivate each of us to fully live life and bin our negative self-talk and fear of failure.

Here is part of a poignant verse written by Nadine Stair, who was eighty-five years old when she composed it. It should be an inspiration to all to grab the gift of life:

If I had my life to live over, I'd dare to make more mistakes next time.

I'd relax. I would limber up. I would be sillier than I have been this trip.

I would take fewer things seriously. I would take more chances.

I would take more trips. I would climb more mountains and swim more rivers.

I would have fewer imaginary troubles.

The central message is that if she had her life over Nadine would not be as fearful. By the age of eighty-five there are, of course, some limitations to what we can do, yet irrespective of our age we can all make positive changes to empower and enrich the rest of our lives. It's highly motivational to occasionally stop and examine your life and beliefs and decide how well they are serving you. Do they hinder you and pull you back or do they help you achieve success, fulfilment and happiness?

Stop, evaluate and reassess what you feel is possible, and make adjustments and new decisions about what you value and treasure. Life is a journey to travel fabulously well.

A few years ago I worked with an inspirational woman called Fiona. A former account manager, at forty-four she started an Open University degree in Human Resources because that's where she saw her future. She knew she was not going to achieve her goal by daydreaming, so she used her friendly inner voice and constantly told herself 'I can do this'.

When she shared her exciting career news with others, one telling response was, 'Really, but you'll have no free time and you'll be approaching fifty before you even get your degree.' Fiona simply smiled and replied in a confident, calm manner, 'Well, as I see it I'll hit fifty years old whatever I do so I might as well be fifty *and* the HR director of a major organisation', and with her confident smile she floated away, leaving the other woman speechless.

EXERCISE

Write your own 'If I had my life to live over' poem

Now it's your turn ... Don't include regrets, just lessons and thoughts to support you in living your best life yet.

Take your time. It's about you so it deserves your 100 per cent attention.

No one else is going to read your verse or list. You are writing this as a gift to yourself, so give it 100 per cent honesty. Trust me, it's an awesomely powerful exercise!

■ Write down the following:

I am _____ (your age now).

If I had my life to live over *now*, I would...

■ Write down as many 'I woulds' as you like – and from all spheres of your life: your well-being, aspirations, career, finances, relationships, achievements, hobbies, education, travel ... The list is endless. What would you go and learn? What would you go and do?

■ Now you have completed your verse, what's your level of motivation right now? How do you feel?

■ What actions will you take as a result of how you feel now? Commit them to paper – record them and write a plan of action. Then follow your plan (go back to Chapter 8 for a recap on turning your dreams and goals into your reality).

Remember that in life two of the greatest motivators are inspiration and desperation. So do you feel inspired because you are living life true to how you want it to be and would you happily press the 'rewind' and 'play' buttons once again...? Or are you feeling desperate because the exercise has exposed for you that you are not living the life you want and you definitely would *not* press replay? Both responses are powerful. The first should spur you on to achieve even more. The latter will no doubt create a spark of desperation that will help you realise that making changes is essential.

Wouldn't it be great if you could say to yourself:

> *'If I had my life to live over, I'd do it in exactly the same way.'*

One year from now, three years from now, ten years from now you will be more disappointed by the FEARs that stopped you taking action, the experiences you didn't have, the opportunities you didn't grab, the risks you didn't take, the doubts you didn't squash than by the things you actually did.

> ❝ The greater danger for most of us is not that our aim is too high and we miss it, but that it is too low and we reach it ❞
>
> **MICHELANGELO**

chapter ten

OPTIMUM ENERGY

Every day of your life is governed by energy; it is all around you and a part of everything you do. People are like magnets and attract energy to them that is positive or negative, high or low voltage. Energy is what you experience when you think of someone special and feel a happy glow, or when you walk into a room and feel bad vibes. The truth is that we are all made up of cosmic energy, as is everything we see, smell, taste and touch.

It is essential to know how to maximise this energy, by liberating it from within as well as attracting it to you from the external world. When you know how to tap into your energy sources you can ensure that it always enhances and never dilutes your day-to-day life.

YOUR MIND IS ENERGY

In Chapter 6 you found out how to use your mind as you would a computer. Well, your mind, just like a computer, needs an energy source. Apparently 13 per cent of calls to computer 'help lines' are from people complaining that their computer isn't working when they haven't actually plugged it in. Don't make the same mistake with your mind – to work at its optimum level it must have a full energy supply.

You are working with high positive energy when you:

- File & Save all your positive and empowering experiences

- Delete & Dump all the negative stuff you don't want to keep

- Mute all negative messages

- Review & Edit your personal experiences and reframe them as positive lessons learnt.

At this stage in the book you should be doing all of the above and experiencing greater energy and enthusiasm as a result. This chapter takes that one step further and shows you how to tap into peak energy states; create and maintain high energy 'batteries'; begin your day in the right frame of mind and end it feeling positive; and how to create a good mood. In other words, you are going to learn how to exercise your mind and get in the best shape possible to give you your best life yet.

LIVE LIFE ON A FULLY CHARGED BATTERY

Imagine that your level of confidence, passion and energy can be measured in the same way as the battery charge on your mobile phone:

- How would you describe your batteries at the moment? Are you living on full, half-full or empty batteries? Do you need to be recharged?

- If you had a battery that measured your confidence and self-belief how charged would that be – full, half full or empty?

- How about your positivity, passion and enthusiasm 'battery' – is it full, half full or on empty?

If you are running on a full battery of positive energy then your mind will be filled with positive ideas, imagination, belief, self-worth and passion. If you feel you are currently running on a low or empty battery then your mind will be low or devoid of these emotions.

INNER STRENGTH

If I asked you, 'How do I get a strong, fit and powerful body?' you'd tell me that physical strength comes from working the muscles of the body to make them strong. Well, inner strength is no different. Think of the mind as a muscle – it needs to be exercised and given a workout to energise it and make it strong and powerful.

If you want to build and strengthen your confidence, belief, self-esteem, positive attitude, courage and determination, the answer is to see these emotions as you would the physical muscles in your body and exercise them. And I don't mean like that once-in-a-blue-moon visit to the gym that we all like to think will do the trick: just like your physical body, your mind requires daily exercising to keep it strong. Regular 'mind workouts' are easy habits to form and you will be delighted at how quickly your inner strength and confidence grow.

> *Confidence is like a muscle*
> *strengthened by continual use.*

MIND WORKOUTS

The following mind workouts bring big results fast. If you decide *not* to take charge of your mind and inner strength, then be very clear that you will not be in charge of your energy, your moods and emotions. You will be living at the mercy of uncontrollable energy surges, high or low, good or bad. I hope you'll agree that this is not an option, so let's look at some fantastic workouts that will get your mind and energy in the best shape ever.

Morning switch-on

The first exercise for your mind every morning is to switch it ON and give yourself a positive power surge immediately after you open your eyes. How you feel first thing each day will greatly influence the way your day unfolds and how you feel about what happens to you throughout the day.

Few people are aware of the need to consciously 'switch on' their positive energy upon waking. They just go with the flow and let external influences and internal thoughts dilute and drain their mind's energy. They greet the day by groaning, 'Oh God is that the time? It can't be time to get up yet...' as they dive back under the duvet. Whatever little energy they had then begins to drain away. If you let your mind run on autopilot and decide to think negative thoughts when you awake then you extinguish your passion and enthusiasm for the day ahead. It's that simple.

Children don't do this. They greet the day with boundless energy and excitement as they jump out of bed, not wanting to miss one second of the exciting things ahead. They don't say 'Oh no, it's raining, the journey to nursery is going to be an absolute nightmare!' They start the day full of positivity and there's no reason why you can't do the same. OK, unlike a child, you may have an idea of what your day has in store but whatever is ahead of you, make sure you start the day well and make the very best of it. It's your day so why waste it by setting yourself up for a bad one and then going through it on automatic pilot. Don't forget those thought boomerangs.

So, how do you achieve a positive frame of mind so you feel invigorated, fully energised and raring to go every day? Try the following success strategy.

Morning questions to kick off a great day

Ask yourself energising and empowering questions the very first thing as you open your eyes each morning – and not those negative ones that can pop into your head un-invited. You can either say them inside your head or out loud. When you do this you pull positive answers and information from the files you have stored in your mind. This is what happens:

- Asking the right questions triggers the right feelings.

- The right feelings trigger the right emotions.

- The right emotions trigger the right actions.

As a result you are the one in control and you make your day exactly as you want it to be: positive, happy, successful and fulfilled.

So get into the habit of asking yourself empowering questions when you wake and as you go through your morning routine, from brushing your teeth to making coffee. Your mind will be active anyway so you may as well be in control of your thoughts instead of letting them wander off wherever they choose.

Awareness is crucial. Know without doubt that your thoughts, questions and answers can set you up for a positive and energised day. Form the habit. Empower yourself.

EXERCISE

Your morning mind workout — the seven-day test

Try asking yourself the following empowering questions first thing in the morning for seven days and notice how your mood and state change for the better. In a short time you won't want to start your day any other way.

■ What am I happy about in my life right now and how does that make me feel?

■ What can I do today that will make me feel more successful, confident, happier and fulfilled?

■ What am I proud of and what have I recently achieved. How does that make me feel?

■ What am I excited and passionate about in my life right now? How does that make me feel?

■ What opportunities are abundant and around me now that will move me towards my goal? How does that make me feel?

■ What am I grateful for in my life right now?

Really connect to the questions and feel the answers – make it a sensory experience with images, colour and sound. (You can of course also write them down.) Adding emotion to your answers will speed up your surge of positive energy. As the week goes on, notice how differently you feel. How much has your positivity, confidence, passion, self-worth and self-belief increased since you started doing this each day?

And if you're worried about fitting this in be assured that I've worked with many busy executives who are also parents and once they tried it out they realised it didn't take even one second of additional time because it's not something to add to your to-do list; it's something you fill your mind with as you get yourself ready for the day.

You're possibly now wondering how, having kept your energy on such a positive high all day, do you switch it off at the end of the evening. Let's look at that next.

Your evening switch-off

Researchers tell us that around 50 per cent of people don't sleep well because they lie there thinking of all the things they should have done, could have done or what went wrong in their day. (If this still sounds familiar to you, please revisit Chapter 7 too.)

In order to sleep soundly you need to get rid of any worrying, negative thoughts and replace them with life-enhancing positive thoughts. Try the following exercise, which will not only ensure you enjoy a blissful night's sleep but also that you wake free from worries.

The aim is to drift off to sleep thinking about all that was right with your day, all you achieved and to feel grateful for it. Do this when you begin winding down – the nearer to sleep time the better. I run through mine as I'm drifting off to sleep or when I'm soaking in a bath at the end of the day.

EXERCISE

Your evening mind workout – the seven-day test

Look back on your day and replay all the good things that have happened by asking yourself empowering questions. Here are some examples:

- What have I done today that has made me feel happy, proud, confident and successful, and how have these experiences made me feel?

- What have I learnt today and how will this help me? How does learning this make me feel?

- What have I felt grateful for today and how has that made me feel?

- What have I achieved today and how did that make me feel?

- What have I done today that was outside my comfort zone and how does this make me feel?

Do this mind workout every night for seven nights and I guarantee you will massively increase your positivity, confidence, belief, enthusiasm and happiness.

Once you've formed the habit of reviewing your day like this you'll sleep in a happy, relaxed, grateful state and wake up with positive energy rather than maybe feeling anxious about the day ahead.

❝ Doing your very best now, in this
moment, puts you in the very best place
for the next moment ❞

OPRAH WINFREY

Evening action replay

If the previous exercise throws up something from your
day you wish had happened differently, or had a more positive outcome, you can address this using an evening action
replay. This involves using your imagination to replay the
experience in your mind as you *wanted* it to go. To do this,
visualise and replay the positive outcome you wanted,
making sure you keep the picture moving like a film. Make
it big, bold and in colour; never a static picture. Use all
your senses and don't forget to add in common sense and a
sense of humour. Store this positive replay to view the next
time you have the opportunity to do something similar and
you'll come at it with a new and positive focus.

Here is one of the most powerful energisers that you
can use at any time of the day. Use it in the morning to
energise yourself and also in the evening to end the day
on a positive high.

EXERCISE

Bucket-loads of gratitude

For this exercise I want you to simply pick one thing
in nature that you really appreciate. A beautiful and
soothing scene is a good choice. The ocean works

every time for me. This will start to clear your mind and balance your energy.

- Visualise and use your imagination to picture a tranquil scene that soothes you. Make it real; the colours, the smells, the noise. The more real you make it the easier it is to connect and still your mind.

- Now focus on all you have that you are grateful for – count your blessings, all of them.

Here's a top tip on gratitude. You must mean it and feel it – never fake it. Connect to what you are grateful for. Be mindful and in the moment. This is one of the most powerful energisers I know.

It is useful to remember that we can easily miss out on experiencing happiness, confidence, self-belief and passion simply by letting the moment pass without stopping to appreciate it. Like making good or bad cakes there's a recipe for creating a happy mood and there's a recipe for miserable moods.

MOOD-MAKING RECIPES

My sister, a trained chef, assures me that to make a great cake you need to mix the right amounts of the right ingredients. It's the same with life. To get a great life you need all the right elements – but it's also possible for that to work in reverse.

The following story illustrates this point. I was visiting one of the London Centrepoint hostels to meet some of the young women living there. One young woman in the group came towards me and said with a massive sigh, 'I'm depressed.'

Now at first this might seem somewhat harsh but what she didn't need was someone saying back to her, 'Oh, so am I and isn't life just the pits,' so my reply was 'Oh hello Depressed … I'm Sharron', accompanied by a big warm smile. She physically moved backwards in amazement as though I had thrown a bucket of water over her, but it got her attention and she agreed to attend one of my Mind Makeover workshops. At the event I explained to her that there is a 'recipe' for creating all emotions, positive or negative, and asked her to tell me how she got so good at creating 'depressed' emotions. Then I would share with her how I got to be so good at creating and making 'happy' emotions. Here is her recipe for 'depressed' emotions and the ingredients she used:

1. First, she said, I had to think of things in the past that had made me deeply unhappy. The worse the experiences, the better I would become at feeling the emotion 'depressed'. And I could dig back years.

2. Now think of the specific people who have let you down and made you feel very unhappy. Picture what happened and replay it over and over again in your mind, remembering how it made you feel. Picture the people and where you were at the time it happened.

3. Next, find a negative person to talk to about it; someone who can help you to feel even worse than you did before you started to talk to them. Grab a

moaner to talk to. Don't worry, she told me, 'there are loads of them'.

4. Finally, she said, you can really speed up the feeling of depressed if you drop your eyes, avoid eye contact with people and stoop and slouch. And, for the cherry on the cake, always speak in a flat, apathetic, monotone voice.

Then, hey presto, you'll have pulled it off and you will be brilliant at being 'depressed'. She closed by telling me that if I practised daily as she did then I would become good at creating depressed feelings really quickly.

I am not a clinical psychologist with the skills to address the unimaginable traumas some of the young women at Centrepoint have experienced – and thankfully this help is available to them. The purpose of my technique is to show the young women how to change habitual ways of negative thinking and being. It returns control to them and motivates them to make positive change, and to break the habitual patterns that dilute their happiness and life.

Good mood recipes

Now let me share my recipe for making happy moods:

- Firstly search in your mind for all the memories you have stored to make you feel happy, confident, ambitious, proud, successful and fulfilled.

- Replay as many of these as possible, real or imaginary, over and over again. See the experience as if it is replaying on an enormous cinema screen in full, bright colour. Make it real and touchable.

- Think of personal experiences in the past when you were in a happy emotional state. Think of the times when your confidence, belief and self-worth were at their highest levels.

- Picture and replay in full colour with high sound. Use all your senses to take you back to that time. Make it as personal as possible.

- Remember how you felt. Who did you share your happiness with that made you feel even better, happier and more proud?

- What was your body language at the time? How did you look? Were you smiling, laughing and excited?

- Repeat and replay these a few times and, hey presto, you'll feel happy. You easily and quickly made a happy mood. Congratulations!

These strategies equip the young women with the ability and belief to start to take their future into their own hands and rebuild it into how they want it to be. That process starts with feeling happier, not miserable or depressed. It starts with focusing with all your will on what is right in your life and not on what is wrong.

The same strategy can work for everyone, irrespective of their starting point.

Later, the young woman who gave me the recipe for creating depressed emotions wrote this on her feedback card: 'I never knew that I was in control of how I feel. It's the best thing I've ever learnt in my life.' She came to another workshop the following year. She had taken all the success tips I had shared with her to heart, focused on her future opportunities and goals, and had enrolled in sixth-form college. She'd just got her A-level results and achieved the grades she needed to start a media course. She said with a beaming smile: 'I'm going to be what I've always wanted to be – a journalist.' Her name is no longer 'Depressed'. Her name is Gillian.

Choose the correct recipe, mix the right ingredients and make the perfect mood and emotions for you and your life. It works every time. What you think, feel and focus on is under your control. With your thoughts you create your mood. Take charge of your mood or it will take charge of you (if it helps think of it this way: mood spelt backwards is doom!).

BEWARE OF EXTERNAL HITS ON YOUR ENERGY

You know with total faith that you are in control of your attitude, thinking and focus. However, the reality of life is that we are surrounded by the external influences of a world filled to bursting with people and their opinions, twenty-four-hour news, entertainment and noise. It's a world that never sleeps.

External influences can be positive or negative but we don't always recognise them as such. It's invaluable to acknowledge and address influencing factors that are diluting your energy and your life. The source could be work, family, home, community, travel, colleagues, friends, TV programmes or films.

Ask yourself the following question on a daily basis. Is my daily life filled with:

- external mood energisers and enhancers that give me personal joy, happiness, success and fulfilment?

or

- external diluters that reduce my personal joy, happiness, success and fulfilment?

Listen carefully to the answers you get.

Often we allow other people's opinions and thoughts to influence us in a way that dilutes our joy. For many people it has simply become habitual to do this. Stop now. These are bad habits and nothing more. You can decide what you want to retain in your life and what to throw out. Decide to bring into your days more life-enhancing habits to empower you. Decide to Dump & Delete old life-diluting and debilitating habits that drain your joy.

We have all met people who offer their negative views and opinions without being asked. These people will dilute your sense of well-being. You may not even know it's happening until it's too late and you start to feel miserable.

> ❝ No one can make you feel second class
> without your permission ❞
>
> **ELEANOR ROOSEVELT**

To demonstrate the diluting power others can have, here's a story I tell at conferences.

Picture this scenario. A beauty consultant – let's call her Sarah – gets up one morning, feeling happy. When she applies her make-up she uses a rather unflattering shade of brown lipstick (fantastic on the catwalk at London's fashion week, but perhaps not so hot for Sarah, as we'll discover). When she arrives at work her closest colleague says 'Are you OK Sarah? You look really pale and washed out.' 'No, I'm good thanks,' says Sarah. Later a second colleague quietly mouths across the counter, 'Sarah are you feeling OK? You don't look so well.' 'No, I'm OK thanks,' says Sarah.

A third colleague and good friend breezes past, smiles and says, 'You look awful; too much vino last night was it?' 'No it was not. I'm fine thank you,' says Sarah in an indignant tone. Sarah had rapidly gone from telling colleagues she was feeling good, then good became OK and OK became fine (remember my mnemonic for FINE?: Frustrated, Insecure, Neurotic and Exhausted…)

So what was going on? Sarah was allowing her positive attitude to the day to be diluted by the negative comments of her colleagues. When a fourth person tells Sarah she looks pale she finally caves in and responds to all the negative energy coming at her: 'You know I really don't feel well at all; maybe I'm getting a bug.' Sarah had allowed negative external influences to change her emotions for the worse so that she actually came to believe that she was feeling unwell. When I tell this story there are howls of laughter and giggles from the audience. Why? For many, it is so true to life.

Of course external energisers can be positive too. Let's change one thing in the story. Picture this scenario, Sarah gets up one morning, feeling happy. When she applies her lipstick she uses a captivating coral shade. (You can tell I've spent years working in cosmetics can't you? I think it's quite normal to say 'captivating' coral!)

At her cosmetic counter her friend and colleague says, 'Wow Sarah you look good this morning.' 'Thanks,' says Sarah, 'I feel really good.' A second colleague with a cheeky grin shouts across the counter: 'You look radiant, what have you been up to?' 'Nothing different,' says Sarah with a smile. Later a third colleague says, 'Hi Sarah, I haven't seen you for ages, you look so well have you been on holiday?' 'No, just feeling great,' says Sarah with an even bigger smile.

The truth is that after three or more positive external influences, which in this example is three people telling us we look good, our emotions change, our confidence and happiness increase, our body language and how we move becomes more confident. We allow these external positive influences to enhance our emotions and our day.

Unless you are acutely aware of your external day-to-day world and the factors that can influence you, you are simply at the mercy of circumstances and everybody else. Remember:

It is your mind and you and you alone are in charge of your thoughts and what you allow in.

Give this some serious thought in the following exercise:

EXERCISE

Negative external influences

- What external influences have you allowed to dilute your success and happiness in the past? Think about other people's opinions, your limiting beliefs, negative self-talk and so on.

- Why did you allow this? When you understand why it becomes much easier and quicker to break the habit and stop doing it.

- What changes can you make in future? What immediate changes will you make? Remember, use the delete and mute commands from Chapter 6. You can change your life in a heartbeat because you can change your thoughts that quickly.

HOW TO FAST-TRACK TO POSITIVE ENERGY

By following the Mind Makeover techniques you will improve your life immeasurably. Here are some supporting techniques you can use to help fast-track you to where you want to get to, personally and professionally. I use all of these in both my day-to-day and working life: they're easy and fun to do and set the best mood for my day ahead.

Read empowering books

You can learn so much from some of the greatest leaders, visionaries, sportspeople and entrepreneurs, and their advice, wisdom and experience is there to be accessed through reading their books. Think about the people who inspire you or visit bookshops and browse through whichever books catch your eye. You will choose the right one for you (you'll find this easy after your Mind Make-over!). I have countless books that have travelled with me for many years and are like trusted friends who support me. The right books can do the same for you.

Meditate

The practice of meditation creates an inner harmony by quietening the mind. It often seems that our thoughts and self-talk come at us at one hundred miles an hour; meditation slows down that constant stream – or at least helps us to observe our thoughts and not became consumed by them. It has a wonderful impact, lowering stress and developing our ability to concentrate wholly on the present. Great things come from silence.

There are many ways to meditate. I practise transcendental meditation to balance my energy and rest my mind after periods of high adrenaline but the choice is a personal one so please invest the time to do some research, and select what will suit you best.

If you've never tried any form of meditation the following technique will give you a flavour of it – and it's so simple you can do two or three minutes of it throughout the day, to step away from the frantic pace of life.

Begin to focus for sixty seconds on your breathing; breathe slowly and deeply, picturing something relaxing and either:

- still your mind and focus on one thing that makes you happy, makes you smile. Keep repeating this. Or

- focus on the only thing that is important now and not all the little stuff. Use your mind to see this one thing going well and with a positive outcome. Keep repeating this.

Do this for even five minutes and you will have positively shifted your energy. This technique is a sanity saver. Focus on the moment and enjoy the now.

We live in a hectic world. Take time to still your mind and give it a break.

Exercise your body

It's the only one you get for your entire life so you need to take care of your precious body. (You can't swap it with someone else's because you like their body more.) And that means exercise – after all, it's what the body is designed to do. Exercise doesn't just keep you physically fit, it's a great way to lift your mood and improve your emotions. When you exercise, you feel positively energised; more relaxed and calm. Your brain releases endorphins, adrenaline, serotonin and dopamine. These chemicals all work together to make you feel good. In addition, after exercising you may feel a sense of accomplishment and your muscles will relax more deeply because of the work-out – easing tension and strain.

Tune into visual power

Switch on to positive visual influencers and energy boost-ers. Some of what is on TV can dilute your positive energy, but lots of channels have feel-good things to watch, includ-ing sport, documentaries and uplifting films.

Choose to watch empowering films and TV channels; go to the theatre to see plays, musicals, dance; visit libraries, art galleries, museums, etc. The list is endless as there's so much to see that is inspiring. When you're inspired you'll feel positively charged and your energy levels will be on full power.

Music

Use music to your advantage. The sheer power of music can give you a massive and immediate positive energy hit and induce exhilarating feelings and moods. A specific piece of music can make you cry or want to dance. It can calm, soothe and relax you, or energise and pump you up and inspire you to take action. Music can also be pro-foundly evocative, have deep resonances and call up spe-cific memories.

All of us have had the experience of being transported by the ability of music to make us feel, act and think a certain way. I use it in business to set a mood. As a confer-ence presenter I can change how the audience feels in an instant by playing a certain piece of music. I remember one particular conference where I hired a professional line-dancing couple to train every person at the conference, from the Global CEO to the new part-time sales associate, to put on their hats and learn to dance. The music helped everyone feel positively energised and to smash out of their comfort zones. The delegates said it was the most fun they'd had in years and it inspired them to carry on growing the company's business by adding a further 27 per cent to the year's turnover.

So now let's put the focus back on you. I've given you many techniques you can use to positively blast your energy levels with the right external influencers. So what are you going to do with this knowledge, because it has no power without you acting on it? What can you do now, today?

Think and be consciously aware of what is it that inspires you and lifts your mood quickly and powerfully. What music, books, pictures, plays, films inspire you? Listen, read, watch … and be inspired.

Create energy-raising mood boards

I hope, having read Chapter 8, that you now have your imagination boards up, and are looking at them often. They are a great way to raise your energy. You can also carry 'mini' boards with you in the form of a notebook, filled with pictures, quotes – anything that lifts your energy and your mood. Or create one on your computer.

Let me share with you my current top five external mood enhancers and energisers (in addition to my motivational books):

1. Pictures of the people I love most, showing positive memories and great life experiences I treasure.

2. A big, full-colour mood board packed with things that inspire me to keep writing my book: a print-out of the book cover, an order form for people to pre-order the book and a mock-up of the book featured in some of my favourite magazines and newspapers (this one I've made up myself to focus on reaching as many people as possible).

3. The project I wrote when I was ten years old (see Chapter 8). The exercise book is opened at the section called 'My Future Life' to remind me that if I see it bold and bright enough and strongly focus on it, then I will, with work and effort, attract it to me.

4. A picture of a goal I'm working towards. Something I want to own and experience. (Don't try to guess what's in my picture but ask yourself 'What's mine going to be?')

5. Favourite quotes I love that give me an immediate energy shift and make me smile. I often put on a daily favourite that is relevant to the energy I want to feel; today's says 'don't wish it was easier, wish you were tougher' which gets me going and motivated!

Whenever I need a mood lift I have just what I need to look at to change how I feel in a moment.

Controlling external influencers and attracting positive energy to you is a decision you make and a choice that requires effort at times. All great things do.

Over to you

What will your five top external mood enhancers and energisers be? Write them down.

Turn up the energy – have fun

Laughter has a huge positive effect on brain chemistry and mood, and is a key stress buster and energiser. Children are experts at having fun and spend most of their days doing just that, so if you want more fun in your life connect to this energy. Laughter is all around us – we simply need to tap into it. If you're going to watch films then watch comedies. If you're going to a club then go to a comedy club. Buy a funny book, read a funny article.

I believe that many of us simply get out of the habit of letting down the boundaries, being silly and finding the humour in things. For years I've bought funny cards for my sister. It's not a big deal but it has a big impact. We are on a lifetime mission to be the one who sent the funniest card. Does being silly make us any less adult or professional? I don't think so. I spend a lot of my time doing pretty daft things – it's fabulous, try it. And if you need inspiration look no further than any young children of your acquaintance and follow their lead.

So let's pull this together. You are energy and your world is energy. Like a magnet you can attract positive, empowering and high energy to you by using the techniques in this chapter. You now have the 'know how' to be in full control and keep your batteries charged. You know how to attract energy to you, and radiate positive energy to others. You have a set of daily exercises to help you get your mind in its best shape yet. Will it take effort? Of course it will and you shouldn't want it any other way. Because with effort comes reward and feelings of personal pride and satisfaction.

Tell yourself:

❝ If it is to be then it's up to me ❞

WILLIAM H. JOHNSON

CONCLUSION

OVER TO YOU

In a novel the author decides the final outcome of the story; not so in *The Mind Makeover*. This book is designed to empower *you*, therefore you are the only one who can decide the outcome of your Mind Makeover – and of course it isn't an ending at all but the beginning of your best life yet!

LIFE IS ABOUT EXPERIENCES NOT POSSESSIONS

At the end of life as we know it, on our last day, should we be asked the question, 'How do you remember your life?' I believe that each of us would sum up our existence by recalling the special moments and experiences we've treasured and shared. We would look back on our memorable life experiences: our contribution to those we love, our family, friends and to society; the lessons we've learnt, the challenges we've overcome, the journeys we took, the destinations we arrived at, the people we've loved and the things we achieved. This is a rich life; a life lived well with passion and gratitude.

I do not believe any of us would sum up our life by reflecting on the material possessions we've amassed: the car we drove, the house we lived in, the money left in our bank account or the wardrobe full of designer clothes. These things do not sum up a life. Experiences and achievements to treasure fill us with immeasurably more happiness, joy and fulfilment than possessions ever will.

Each of us wants to live a passionate and fulfilling life, yet sometimes we let our day-to-day responsibilities hold us back. We stop believing that we are responsible for our own destiny and that we *can* make things happen. There is no time like the present to feel happy, successful and fulfilled. So start now and take bold action because the techniques I've shared with you in *The Mind Makeover* are life-affirming and, most importantly, life-transforming – but only if you use them. Take ownership, commit and do it now.

After experiencing a Mind Makeover many individuals smash out of their comfort zones and habitual ways of being and doing, stretch their imagination and break the boundaries of what they previously believed was possible. As a result, they go on to achieve happiness, success and fulfilment way beyond their wildest dreams. They imagine abundance, see abundance and feel abundance and so they experience abundance in all areas of their life. I'm describing *you* here.

BE MINDFUL – LIVE IN THE MOMENT

Be present and focus all your attention on what you are doing and thinking in each moment. Fully commit to seizing all the moments that give you joy throughout your day. Why wait for your annual holiday to appreciate a sunset, sunrise, full moon or a rainbow? Why wait to feel grateful for a friend's support, a funny thing that's happened, an opportunity right there for you to seize, the choices you have, the people you know ... Stop and appreciate all that's right precisely when it is right and in that very moment. Decide to be present in your own life. Do this as much as you can and as often as you can as it will enrich your life immeasurably. It's said that yesterday is history, tomorrow is a mystery and today is the present. That's why each day of life is a gift.

FEEL THE WIND ON YOUR BACK

There are times in our life when we feel that we have the wind behind us, gently supporting and pushing us forward towards our goals. But there are also times when we feel the wind is in front of us, pushing us backwards and away from our goals and desires – sometimes with the strength of a force-ten gale. Whether you feel you are being propelled forward or held back, I want you to know that you now have all you need to push forward to your best life yet, if you use your motivation, determination and persistence to take massive action. When I was writing this book I had times when it felt like that force-ten gale was against me and I also experienced many times when a gentle breeze was pushing me forward. Trust me, I was far more driven to succeed when faced with the force-ten gale. Why? Because not achieving my goal was not an option. Make this the same for you, whatever your goal.

YOUR FUTURE STARTS NOW

The only threat to your future success is indecision, so decide with all your heart what it is you want to have, be and do. You now know how to predict your future – create it.

> 6 Go confidently in the direction of your dreams! Live the life you've imagined 9
>
> **THOREAU**

Make up your mind *now* about:

- What you want

- Why you want it

- How you're going to get it.

Whatever success and fulfilment mean to you, and only you can decide, by using the principles in this book you can make a positive impact on every area of your life, be it career, relationships, well-being, confidence or finances. Your levels of happiness, success, fulfilment and simply your 'joy of life' can and will increase to a new all-time high.

Have unwavering belief that it's your world and your future is in your hands. You are the creator of your destiny so it's up to you to use your mind to empower you to live the life you've imagined. And, as you do, be your own best friend every day of the journey – a friend to support, guide, encourage and challenge you to give your best and be your best. Treat your thoughts as though your entire world revolves around them, because, as you know with absolute faith, your whole world *does* revolve around them. With your thoughts you create your world.

Be unique and be yourself – you are fabulous! Celebrate and be grateful for all that's good in your life right now and watch your life getting better and better day after day. Use your Mind Makeover to move you towards living your best life yet. Your future starts here and now with the controls and responsibility for your life exactly where they should be – firmly in your own hands. It's all there waiting for you to seize the moment and all the opportunities that life has to offer.

Your time is now so write your own ending to *The Mind Makeover*: make it fabulous and remember always that you are too!

INDEX